Progress in Grammar, Punctuation and Spelling Assessment

MANUAL STAGE 1
Years 1–2

◆MARK

RS✱ASSESSMENT
FROM **HODDER EDUCATION**

Although every effort has been made to ensure that website addresses are correct at time of going to press, RS Assessment from Hodder Education cannot be held responsible for the content of any website mentioned in this book. It is sometimes possible to find a relocated web page by typing in the address of the home page for a website in the URL window of your browser.

Orders: please contact Bookpoint Ltd, 130 Park Drive, Milton Park, Abingdon, Oxon OX14 4SE. Telephone: (44) 01235 400555. Email: primary@bookpoint.co.uk.

Lines are open from 9 a.m. to 5 p.m., Monday to Saturday, with a 24-hour message answering service. Visit our website at www.rsassessment.com for details of other assessment publications.

Online support and queries email: onlinesupport@rsassessment.com

ISBN: 978 1 47188 503 7

© Rising Stars UK Ltd 2018

First published in 2018 by
RS Assessment from Hodder Education, part of the Hodder Education Group
An Hachette UK Company
Carmelite House
50 Victoria Embankment
London EC4Y 0DZ

www.rsassessment.com

Impression number   10 9 8 7 6 5 4 3

Year   2022 2021 2020 2019

Progress in Grammar, Punctuation and Spelling Assessment developed by Alpha*Plus* Consultancy Ltd.

Author and review team: Annabel Charles, Becky Clarkson, Alissa McDonald, Claire Metcalfe, Kate Ruttle, Romy Short, Siobhan Skeffington.

All rights reserved. Apart from any use permitted under UK copyright law, the material in this publication is copyright and cannot be photocopied or otherwise produced in its entirety or copied onto acetate without permission. Electronic copying is not permitted. Permission is given to teachers to make copies of individual pages marked © Rising Stars UK Ltd 2018. You may photocopy this sheet, for classroom distribution only, to pupils within their own school or educational institution. The material may not be copied in unlimited quantities, kept on behalf of others, distributed outside the purchasing institution, copied onwards, sold to third parties, or stored for future use in a retrieval system. This permission is subject to the payment of the purchase price of the book. If you wish to use the material in any way other than as specified you must apply in writing to the Publisher at the above address.

Typeset in India

Printed in the UK

A catalogue record for this title is available from the British Library.

Contents

1 Introduction — 5
- Why use *GaPS*? — 5
- Curriculum maps and progression in *GaPS* — 6
- *GaPS* online analysis and reports — 7
- Monitoring and predicting progress using *GaPS* — 7
- When to use each *GaPS* test — 8
- Performance indicators — 8
- Who can you assess using *GaPS*? — 9

2 Administering the *GaPS* tests — 10
- When to test — 10
- Group size — 10
- Timing — 10
- Preparation — 10
- Administering the test — 10
- Spelling test transcripts — 11

3 Answers and mark schemes — 18
- Marking the answers — 18
- Finding the total raw score — 18
- Profiling performance by strand — 18
- Obtaining other scores — 18
- Answers and mark schemes for each test (including facilities for each question) — 20
- Record Sheet for each test (photocopiable) — 48

4 Test scores — 50
- Summative measures — 50
- Diagnostic and formative interpretation — 55
- Reporting progress using the Hodder Scale — 56
- Predicting future performance with the Hodder Scale — 56
- Case studies — 58

5 Technical information — 60
- Standardisation sample — 60
- Reliability — 60
- Validity — 62

6 Standardised score tables — 63
- Standardised scores, Hodder Scale scores and GPS ages for *GaPS* — 63
- Age-standardised scores for *GaPS* — 69

Acknowledgements

The authors and publishers would like to thank the staff and pupils from the following schools that took part in trialling in Autumn 2016 and Spring and Summer 2017.

Alderman Cogan's Church of England Primary Academy, Hull

All Saints Primary School Runcorn, Runcorn

Anglesey Primary School, Burton-upon-Trent

Castleton Primary School, Leeds

Cedar Children's Academy, Rochester

Dean Bank Primary and Nursery School, Ferryhill

Denbigh Primary School, Luton

Emmer Green Primary School, Reading

Garswood Primary and Nursery School, Garswood

Madley Primary School, Hereford

The Marist Catholic Primary School, West Byfleet

Marhamchurch CofE VC Primary School, Marhamchurch

Markington CE Primary School, Markington

Melbury Primary School, Nottingham

Moortown Primary School, Leeds

Our Lady of the Rosary RC VA Primary School, Bristol

Penn Wood Primary and Nursery School, Slough

Riverside Community Primary School and Nursery, Plymouth

Saints Peter and Paul Catholic Primary School, Coventry

Scholes (Elmet) Primary School, Leeds

Springfield Primary School, Derby

St. Anselm's Catholic Primary School, Harrow

St. Charles RC Primary School, Blackburn

St. Edmund's Roman Catholic Primary School, Manchester

St. James' Church of England Primary School, Wetherby

St. John's CE (C) Primary School, Keele

St. Joseph's Preparatory School, Stoke-on-Trent

St. Mary Cray Primary Academy, Orpington

St. Paul's CE Primary School, Salford

St. White's Primary School, Cinderford

Trowell CofE Primary School, Nottingham

Vauxhall Primary School, London

The Westborough School, Southend-on-Sea

Woodland View Junior School, Norwich

1 Introduction

Progress in Grammar, Punctuation and Spelling (GaPS) provides a termly standardised assessment of a pupil's English language and spelling attainment, plus a profile of grammar, punctuation, vocabulary and spelling skills, which helps you identify those pupils who may need further teaching and practice. Separate tests are available for the Autumn, Spring and Summer terms for each of Years 1 to 6. *GaPS* is designed for whole-class use, with pupils of all abilities. The *GaPS* tests are designed to be used just after half-term, but may also be used towards the end of each term in each primary school year in order to measure and monitor pupils' progress and to provide reliable predictive and diagnostic information. The tests are simple and quick to administer, and straightforward to mark. Each test takes between 40 and 50 minutes, depending on the year group, and each test is divided into two parts – one for grammar, punctuation and vocabulary and the other for spelling – which can be administered separately.

GaPS tests assess the 2014 National Curriculum and the content domain-assessable elements of the 2015 English grammar, punctuation and spelling test frameworks published by the Standards and Testing Agency for National Curriculum Tests. The *GaPS* tests provide thorough coverage of the National Curriculum 2014 Programme of Study for each year. This has been assured by systematically sampling Key Stage 1 and Key Stage 2 performance descriptors for English using the 2015 test frameworks and being informed by the Key Stage 1 and Key Stage 2 national tests.

A large-scale standardisation trial (involving over 30 schools and over 6000 pupils) was undertaken for *GaPS* between September 2016 and July 2017, with nationally representative groups of pupils, to produce the data tables provided in this manual. This enables schools to have confidence in the information provided from these new tests. Further details about this process are provided in Chapter 5 *Technical information*.

Why use *GaPS*?

Using *GaPS* provides many benefits. First, *GaPS* gives reliable summative information, for example:

- if you want to follow the progress of your pupils from term to term, as well as year to year through the primary school, *GaPS* provides *three* carefully designed tests for each year;
- if you wish to set appropriate and meaningful targets for your pupils, and to evaluate their progress, *GaPS* tests provide an empirical basis on which to do so;
- if you need to have an external reference for your value-added requirements, *GaPS* tests supply it.

Second, *GaPS* also has a diagnostic capability, enabling you to investigate the strengths and weaknesses of your pupils' language skills across grammar, punctuation, vocabulary and spelling.

Table 1.1 Strands used in *GaPS*

Strand	Description
G	Grammar
P	Punctuation
V	Vocabulary
S	Spelling

You can also examine the performance of pupils on each question. Using the percentage of pupils who answered each question correctly in the national standardisation (the facility value), you can easily compare the performance of your own pupils with those in the national sample. You will find facility values by each question in the relevant mark scheme.

GaPS will help you answer parents, governors, inspectors or headteachers who ask the following questions:

- How has *my* child done compared to others of his/her age or year group?
- What pattern of performance do pupils in a particular year typically achieve?
- Has this pupil made good progress from year to year?
- What would be a reasonable level of achievement for this pupil next term?
- What are the strengths of this pupil, or class?
- What individual and class *targets* are appropriate and realistic?
- On what aspects of language should this pupil focus to maximise progress?
- What would constitute good, average or poor progress for this pupil, or class?
- What is my child's GPS age?

This manual contains all the information you need to obtain standardised scores, age-standardised scores, percentiles, grammar, punctuation, vocabulary and spelling age, a score on the Hodder Scale together with age-related performance indicators for the end of year and a profile of performance against strands. All together, the various scores provide a wealth of information that will support you in managing learning in your classroom.

Curriculum maps and progression in *GaPS*

The *GaPS* tests provide thorough coverage of the National Curriculum 2014 Programme of Study for the particular year.

The *GaPS* curriculum maps (available for free at www.risingstars-uk.com/gaps-curriculum-maps) take in the 2014 Programme of Study, which describes what should be covered by the end of each year, and how the teaching of the material might be allocated to each term. For a test to give reliable results, it needs to be valid – that is, to assess what has been taught – so the curriculum maps define what *GaPS* assesses each term.

The *GaPS* curriculum map for each term will help in planning your teaching. The curriculum maps have been designed to break down the national curriculum into a meaningful term-by-term programme of study, breaking down skills and content into termly 'chunks'. These maps have been designed so that skills and content get progressively more difficult over the terms and years of Key Stage 1. Similarly the tests have been designed to assess this progressively more difficult content and to build upon assessments from the previous terms and years. The maps are designed to cover all necessary content in a meaningful progression so that pupils are at the expected point in their learning when they reach the end of Key Stage 1 national tests.

GaPS online analysis and reports

If you are using the pencil-and-paper tests, the online analysis and reporting tool on MARK (My Assessment and Reporting Kit) will enable you to analyse group performance (for example, by class and/or gender), track pupil performance through the school and generate individual progress predictions. See page 19 for more information.

Monitoring and predicting progress using *GaPS*

GaPS tests give you five distinct types of information to inform you of the progress of each child, class and cohort:

- **standardised scores**, which show how a learner's score relates to national performance;
- **age-standardised scores**, which take into account a child's chronological age so that you can see how a child's performance compares with other children of the same age;
- **grammar, punctuation, vocabulary and spelling age** for a quick at-a-glance reference;
- **performance indicators**, giving relative attainment term on term;
- the **Hodder Scale**, which is an independent measure of progress throughout primary.

The use of each of these scores is explained more fully in Chapter 4 *Test scores*.

The *GaPS* test results have been statistically linked from term to term and year to year, to allow progress to be measured across the different terms and years. Results from the test enable you to monitor strengths and weaknesses and track progress through the whole primary phase. The information provided in this manual enables you to monitor and compare in detail individual patterns of performance against the norms and patterns for the term or year.

The Hodder Scale acts as a common 'spine' on which are plotted all of the *GaPS* tests across the whole primary phase (Table 4.5 on page 57 shows this scale across Key Stage 1). It provides the statistical basis for predicting pupil progress and future attainment, based on the termly performance data of over 6000 pupils nationally.

The Hodder Scale, as a fixed reference point, has the virtue of being a secure standard with a proven history. It is directly related to the raw scores in *GaPS* and does not take age into account. Teachers can use the results from a *GaPS* test, the Hodder Scale, age-standardised scores and standardised score information together with the performance indicator band to provide clear evidence of how well pupils are doing with their grammar, punctuation and spelling from term to term.

Many teachers wish to be able to use the results from *GaPS* tests to find out if their pupils are working at the expected standard for the term. This information can be calculated from the standardised score, using the bands in Table 1.2 on page 8.

Profiling test scores

The photocopiable *GaPS* Record Sheets on pages 48–49 will enable you to profile scores and analyse pupils' performance in the different grammar, punctuation and spelling strands. You can then evaluate their progress relative to national average performance (shown by the tints) for each aspect of grammar, punctuation and spelling to see if there are patterns of strengths and weaknesses. (See 'Profiling performance by strand' on page 18 for further details.)

You may also go one stage further and check a pupil's individual performance on a specific question and compare how they have performed relative to other pupils in the same year group. Refer to the mark scheme to see what proportion of pupils in that year group answered each question correctly. This is called the *facility* and is shown as a percentage: 60 per cent shows that 60 per cent of pupils in the national sample answered the question correctly.

If you wish, you can also average your pupils' scores to create an overall *class or cohort* profile. The pattern revealed may inform both teaching and target setting, as it will highlight the GPS skills in which pupils are secure or confident and those that need further support and practice. Alternatively, input the scores into MARK for automatic profile reporting (see page 19).

When to use each *GaPS* test

GaPS provides the most useful information if it is used termly. However, if necessary, it can be used just once every year. The tests for years 1 and 2 each contain 40 marks with all the tests assessing different elements from the national curriculum. Section A of each test includes a range of questions assessing grammar, punctuation and vocabulary relevant to each term as set out in the *GaPS* curriculum map. Section B of each test assesses spelling rules and words from the word list set out in the curriculum map. The tests should be taken when the relevant content has been taught; this may vary depending on the school's own schemes of work. The tests are designed to be used just after half-term, but may also be used towards the end of each term in each primary school year in order to provide reliable information.

The Key Stage 1 *GaPS* tests are able to provide a profile of the performance of your pupils in the core skills and content that underpin progress in grammar, punctuation, vocabulary and spelling, enabling you to focus your attention on supporting them as they develop the most important skills.

Performance indicators

The performance indicators reflect where pupils, groups, classes and the schools are in relation to other schools term on term. We have developed the following performance indicators to provide you with information about relative performance each term.

Table 1.2 Performance indicator bands

Performance indicator	Standardised score
Working towards	<94
Working at	94–114
Working at greater depth	>114

This measure is based on the standards calculated from the performance of our national representative standardisation sample. The standardisation has set the average score at 100, with 15 marks each side of this being one standard deviation. That is 68% of pupils would fall between a standardised score of 85 and 115. The levels set here are set such that schools are expected to generally be better than the national average. This is to ensure that they are on track to achieve the required standards at Key Stage 1. The 'working at greater depth' standard is set so that 16% of learners will achieve this.

Children with standardised scores just below or just above 94–95 may be considered on the cusp of the performance indicator band. The performance of children on the cusp is always less predictable than those who achieve scores comfortably within the expected standard. We want to ensure that we don't overinflate the performance of children on the cusp, so we have set the performance indicator band for 'Working at' to be slightly more demanding than the national test expected standard.

These performance indicator bands may be used for tests in each term to measure if a child is on track to achieve an expected standard at the end of the year and to aggregate performance for groups, classes and years. These performance indicators will be available as part of the online analysis and reporting service (see page 19 for more information).

If a child achieves the 'working at greater depth' performance indicator band in a test, they won't necessarily be predicted 'working at greater depth' in the next test. This is because the Hodder scale score table is based on actual pupil performance and this pattern shows that children with similar performances sometimes fall below the 'working at greater depth' band on the next test. This seems to be prevalent for Autumn to Spring predictions. In Autumn there is recap of the previous year's curriculum, whereas the Spring test will have more questions of the current year's curriculum. There may also be more questions at greater depth within the Spring curriculum, meaning that the Spring test provides a greater challenge. In any given test only a few marks will fall within the 'working at greater depth' performance indicator band, so the judgement of 'working at greater depth' has to be seen as indicative rather than totally secure. For a secure judgement of 'working at greater depth' there needs to be a greater array of evidence.

Who can you assess using *GaPS*?

The spread of demand of the tests allows you to use each test with wide-ability groups, including weaker pupils, and allows all pupils to experience some success.

Very low attaining pupils may benefit from taking tests intended for earlier terms or years, where they are more likely to experience success and be able to demonstrate what they know and understand, rather than struggle with questions that are too demanding for them. In a similar way, high attaining pupils following an extension or accelerated pathway may take tests intended for older age groups, which will provide evidence of them working at greater depth as they will meet more difficult questions.

Please note that it may not be possible to obtain an age-standardised score or percentile when the tests are used in this way, if the pupil is outside the chronological age range of the conversion table for the test used. However, you may be able to get a GPS age, and will be able to get a Hodder Scale score.

2 Administering the *GaPS* tests

When to test

The *GaPS* tests should ideally be used shortly after the relevant half-term, since this exactly mirrors the time they were taken in the trialling and will therefore give the most dependable data. However, in practice, using the tests one or two months either side of this optimum point is unlikely to be critical. This pattern also provides objective information for the pupil progress meetings and data-collection points which most schools have at around half-term.

Using the *GaPS* tests earlier rather than later in the second half of term can help the results to feed into and inform classroom practice or be used for end-of-term reporting.

Group size

You can administer the tests to whole classes or large groups if you feel comfortable doing so. With younger children, however, it may be better to administer the tests in small groups supported by a teaching assistant.

Timing

A maximum time limit of 40 minutes is set for the Key Stage 1 *GaPS* tests. The grammar, punctuation and vocabulary section of the test is likely to take 20 minutes. The spelling test will take between 15 and 20 minutes. You may want to allow a break between the two sections of the test.

Preparation

Each pupil will need a copy of the appropriate test booklet plus a pencil or pen and an eraser. Answers may be altered by crossing or rubbing out.

Administering the test

Ask pupils to write their name, gender, date of birth and test date on the front of the test booklet. If any pupils are not clear about what they have to do, you may give additional explanation to help them understand the requirements of the test. If a child needs further help you may read the Section A questions aloud but do not help with individual words. If they are unable to understand they should move on to the next question.

If the results are to be reliable, it is important that the pupils work alone, without copying from each other or discussing their answers.

Before pupils complete Section A of the test (grammar, punctuation and vocabulary), explain the following key points to them:

- the answer booklet consists of a range of questions: children should attempt them all;

- if children find a question too hard, they should have a go and then move on to the next one: they should not spend too long on questions they cannot answer;
- if children have problems, they should ask for help by raising their hand;
- children have approximately 20 minutes to complete the first part of the test;
- if they finish before then, they should go back and check their work.

After pupils have completed Section A of the test move on to Section B (spelling). You may wish to administer this after the children have had a break. Ensure that all children are on the correct page in their test booklet and explain the following key points:

- that for the spelling section of the test you are going to read out 20 sentences to them;
- each sentence has a word missing on their answer sheet;
- they should listen carefully to the missing word and write the word, making sure they spell it correctly, on the line within the sentence in their test booklets;
- you will read the word, then the word within a sentence and then repeat the word a third time.

Spelling test transcripts

Pages 12–17 contain the transcripts for the spelling tests which you should read aloud. There are 20 words in the test. You should introduce each word with the sentence 'The word is "xxx"'. Then read the sentence with the word included in the sentence and then finally repeat the sentence 'The word is "xxx"'.

GaPS 1 Autumn Spelling test transcript

Qn	Teacher script
1	Spelling 1: The picture shows a **fish**. The word is **fish**.
2	Spelling 2: The picture shows a **coin**. The word is **coin**.
3	Spelling 3: The picture shows a **hand**. The word is **hand**.
4	Spelling 4: The word is **off**. I took my coat **off**. The word is **off**.
5	Spelling 5: The word is **mess**. Your room is a **mess**. The word is **mess**.
6	Spelling 6: The word is **sank**. My boot **sank** into the mud. The word is **sank**.
7	Spelling 7: The word is **have**. They **have** gone swimming. The word is **have**.
8	Spelling 8: The word is **my**. We live in the same town as **my** grandad. The word is **my**.
9	Spelling 9: The word is **helping**. I like **helping** my sister. The word is **helping**.
10	Spelling 10: The word is **rain**. Sam got wet in the **rain**. The word is **rain**.
11	Spelling 11: The word is **was**. I **was** playing with my toys. The word is **was**.
12	Spelling 12: The word is **see**. I can **see** a bus. The word is **see**.
13	Spelling 13: The word is **boat**. The **boat** was on the pond. The word is **boat**.
14	Spelling 14: The word is **zoo**. There is a lion in the **zoo**. The word is **zoo**.
15	Spelling 15: The word is **join**. I want to **join** the game. The word is **join**.
16	Spelling 16: The word is **clown**. The **clown** had a red nose. The word is **clown**.
17	Spelling 17: The word is **today**. We went shopping **today**. The word is **today**.
18	Spelling 18: The word is **said**. The teacher **said** we could read. The word is **said**.
19	Spelling 19: The word is **pie**. Bella ate beef **pie**. The word is **pie**.
20	Spelling 20: The word is **nose**. The man had a long **nose**. The word is **nose**.

GaPS 1 *Spring* Spelling test transcript

Qn	Teacher script
1	Spelling 1: The word is **love**. I **love** to sing. The word is **love**.
2	Spelling 2: The word is **arm**. She has a cut on her **arm**. The word is **arm**.
3	Spelling 3: The word is **played**. They **played** tennis. The word is **played**.
4	Spelling 4: The word is **some**. There are **some** sheep in the field. The word is **some**.
5	Spelling 5: The word is **her**. He gave **her** a book. The word is **her**.
6	Spelling 6: The word is **skin**. My **skin** felt smooth. The word is **skin**.
7	Spelling 7: The word is **bird**. The **bird** was in the cage. The word is **bird**.
8	Spelling 8: The word is **fair**. They sold candy floss at the **fair**. The word is **fair**.
9	Spelling 9: The word is **one**. There is **one** muffin left. The word is **one**.
10	Spelling 10: The word is **helped**. We **helped** tidy the classroom. The word is **helped**.
11	Spelling 11: The word is **bear**. I cuddle my **bear** at bedtime. The word is **bear**.
12	Spelling 12: The word is **party**. The children went to a **party**. The word is **party**.
13	Spelling 13: The word is **short**. Jack had very **short** trousers. The word is **short**.
14	Spelling 14: The word is **hear**. We can **hear** the wind. The word is **hear**.
15	Spelling 15: The word is **saw**. I **saw** the kite. The word is **saw**.
16	Spelling 16: The word is **when**. The dog sleeps **when** he is tired. The word is **when**.
17	Spelling 17: The word is **once**. I have only been to the seaside **once**. The word is **once**.
18	Spelling 18: The word is **care**. I will **care** for my rabbit. The word is **care**.
19	Spelling 19: The word is **come**. I can **come** to the cinema. The word is **come**.
20	Spelling 20: The word is **August**. In **August** we go on holiday. The word is **August**.

GaPS 1 Summer Spelling test transcript

Qn	Teacher script
1	Spelling 1: The word is **book**. I read the **book**. The word is **book**.
2	Spelling 2: The word is **pull**. I can **pull** the rope. The word is **pull**.
3	Spelling 3: The word is **wheel**. The **wheel** kept spinning. The word is **wheel**.
4	Spelling 4: The word is **dolphin**. The **dolphin** swam in the sea. The word is **dolphin**.
5	Spelling 5: The word is **birds**. The **birds** were singing in the trees. The word is **birds**.
6	Spelling 6: The word is **washes**. Tim **washes** his face. The word is **washes**.
7	Spelling 7: The word is **bread**. The **bread** had cheese on top. The word is **bread**.
8	Spelling 8: The word is **there**. My coat is over **there**. The word is **there**.
9	Spelling 9: The word is **Friday**. **Friday** is my favourite day. The word is **Friday**.
10	Spelling 10: The word is **farmyard**. The chickens were in the **farmyard**. The word is **farmyard**.
11	Spelling 11: The word is **blackberry**. We ate **blackberry** and apple crumble. The word is **blackberry**.
12	Spelling 12: The word is **football**. My mum watched the **football**. The word is **football**.
13	Spelling 13: The word is **playground**. We played tag in the **playground**. The word is **playground**.
14	Spelling 14: The word is **friend**. My **friend** is going to the circus with me. The word is **friend**.
15	Spelling 15: The word is **under**. The woodlouse lives **under** the stone. The word is **under**.
16	Spelling 16: The word is **put**. I **put** my bag by the door. The word is **put**.
17	Spelling 17: The word is **push**. Jane can **push** the swing. The word is **push**.
18	Spelling 18: The word is **school**. I take my lunch box to **school**. The word is **school**.
19	Spelling 19: The word is **house**. The **house** was on top of the hill. The word is **house**.
20	Spelling 20: The word is **full**. My bowl is **full** of cereal. The word is **full**.

GaPS 2 Autumn Spelling test transcript

Qn	Teacher script
1	Spelling 1: The word is **very**. The cup is **very** full. The word is **very**.
2	Spelling 2: The word is **catch**. Rama can **catch** a ball. The word is **catch**.
3	Spelling 3: The word is **think**. I **think** my school is great. The word is **think**.
4	Spelling 4: The word is **cold**. It is **cold** when it snows. The word is **cold**.
5	Spelling 5: The word is **dry**. Our paintings were left to **dry**. The word is **dry**.
6	Spelling 6: The word is **kind**. It is very **kind** to share our toys. The word is **kind**.
7	Spelling 7: The word is **ice**. Water can turn into **ice**. The word is **ice**.
8	Spelling 8: The word is **babies**. The **babies** made lots of noise. The word is **babies**.
9	Spelling 9: The word is **kicking**. Jack was **kicking** the ball into the goal. The word is **kicking**.
10	Spelling 10: The word is **fixed**. Sam **fixed** his broken model. The word is **fixed**.
11	Spelling 11: The word is **race**. Josh won the skipping **race**. The word is **race**.
12	Spelling 12: The word is **wanted**. Simon **wanted** to write a story. The word is **wanted**.
13	Spelling 13: The word is **magic**. Sarah loves to do **magic** tricks. The word is **magic**.
14	Spelling 14: The word is **child**. Every **child** should be kept safe. The word is **child**.
15	Spelling 15: The word is **talking**. My teacher was **talking** about healthy food. The word is **talking**.
16	Spelling 16: The word is **fiction**. I love to read **fiction** books. The word is **fiction**.
17	Spelling 17: The word is **usual**. The school bell rang earlier than **usual**. The word is **usual**.
18	Spelling 18: The word is **bridge**. Class two designed a **bridge**. The word is **bridge**.
19	Spelling 19: The word is **dropped**. Setsuko **dropped** her seeds into the pot. The word is **dropped**.
20	Spelling 20: The word is **clothes**. Ali put his **clothes** in the suitcase. The word is **clothes**.

GaPS 2 Spring Spelling test transcript

Qn	Teacher script
1	Spelling 1: The word is **jog**. I like to **jog** around the football field. The word is **jog**.
2	Spelling 2: The word is **ball**. Chen kicked the **ball**. The word is **ball**.
3	Spelling 3: The word is **key**. Seb unlocked the door with a **key**. The word is **key**.
4	Spelling 4: The word is **cars**. Polly played with her toy **cars**. The word is **cars**.
5	Spelling 5: The word is **talk**. We should not **talk** to strangers. The word is **talk**.
6	Spelling 6: The word is **city**. New York is an amazing **city**. The word is **city**.
7	Spelling 7: The word is **Mrs**. Ben's teacher is called **Mrs** Smith. The word is **Mrs**.
8	Spelling 8: The word is **above**. The aeroplane flew in the sky **above** us. The word is **above**.
9	Spelling 9: The word is **badly**. Nisha fell and hurt her leg **badly**. The word is **badly**.
10	Spelling 10: The word is **wild**. Lions live in the **wild**. The word is **wild**.
11	Spelling 11: The word is **Monday**. We go back to school on a **Monday**. The word is **Monday**.
12	Spelling 12: The word is **hasn't**. The seed **hasn't** started to grow. The word is **hasn't**.
13	Spelling 13: The word is **station**. The train stopped at the **station**. The word is **station**.
14	Spelling 14: The word is **carries**. A postman **carries** his letters in a bag. The word is **carries**.
15	Spelling 15: The word is **shopping**. Jemal helped his dad do the **shopping**. The word is **shopping**.
16	Spelling 16: The word is **because**. Kate got wet **because** it was raining. The word is **because**.
17	Spelling 17: The word is **pretty**. Marcus painted a **pretty** flower. The word is **pretty**.
18	Spelling 18: The word is **glove**. Wissam put his **glove** in his pocket. The word is **glove**.
19	Spelling 19: The word is **always**. A square **always** has four edges. The word is **always**.
20	Spelling 20: The word is **happily**. Cinderella lived **happily** ever after. The word is **happily**.

GaPS 2 Summer Spelling test transcript

Qn	Teacher script
1	Spelling 1: The word is **small**. Jake's new kitten is really **small**. The word is **small**.
2	Spelling 2: The word is **I'm**. I can watch the film if **I'm** good. The word is **I'm**.
3	Spelling 3: The word is **bath**. George has a **bath** every night. The word is **bath**.
4	Spelling 4: The word is **bushes**. Some animals live in **bushes**. The word is **bushes**.
5	Spelling 5: The word is **money**. Hassan is saving his pocket **money**. The word is **money**.
6	Spelling 6: The word is **apple**. An **apple** fell from the tree. The word is **apple**.
7	Spelling 7: The word is **work**. Nisha tried hard to finish her **work**. The word is **work**.
8	Spelling 8: The word is **pencil**. Ben dropped his **pencil** on the floor. The word is **pencil**.
9	Spelling 9: The word is **donkey**. A young **donkey** is called a foal. The word is **donkey**.
10	Spelling 10: The word is **know**. All children need to **know** how to read. The word is **know**.
11	Spelling 11: The word is **warm**. Anna sat by the fire to keep **warm**. The word is **warm**.
12	Spelling 12: The word is **should**. We **should** be kind to animals. The word is **should**.
13	Spelling 13: The word is **petal**. Megan pulled a **petal** off the flower. The word is **petal**.
14	Spelling 14: The word is **sadness**. Joe felt full of **sadness**. The word is **sadness**.
15	Spelling 15: The word is **knock**. It is polite to **knock** on the door. The word is **knock**.
16	Spelling 16: The word is **towel**. Tom used his **towel** to dry himself. The word is **towel**.
17	Spelling 26: The word is **beautiful**. Emma wandered round the **beautiful** garden. The word is **beautiful**.
18	Spelling 18: The word is **people**. Hundreds of **people** watched the football match. The word is **people**.
19	Spelling 19: The word is **enjoyment**. Mina's party was filled with **enjoyment**. The word is **enjoyment**.
20	Spelling 20: The word is **write**. Robert loves to **write** stories. The word is **write**.

3 Answers and mark schemes

Once the pupil has completed a *GaPS* test, their answers may be marked using the answers and mark schemes found in this chapter.

Marking the answers

- Use the score box in the right-hand margin alongside each question in the test booklets to record marks.
- Please use your professional judgement when marking.
- Any clear indication of the answer is acceptable irrespective of what was asked for, e.g. a tick or a circle. If more answers than required have been circled or ticked, the mark should not be awarded except if it is clearly indicated that an incorrect response was initially made and then corrected.

Finding the total raw score

You can record total marks for the page at the bottom of each page in the test booklets. Then add together the page scores to find each pupil's total raw score and record this in the total marks box on the front cover.

Profiling performance by strand

A code beneath each mark box in Section A indicates which strand the question is assessing: grammar (G), punctuation (P) or vocabulary (V). The questions in Section B all assess spelling so have not been coded. The *GaPS* curriculum maps (see page 6) provide details of the content allocation of the strands per year and term. The mark schemes also include the STA national test framework code(s) (available from www.gov.uk/government/collections/national-curriculum-assessments-test-frameworks) for each question so that you can see test performance at a more granular level. For *GaPS*, code G6.5 has been added and used for Section A questions assessing homophones and near homophones (Years 1–4) and homophones and other words that are often confused (Years 5 and 6).

If you wish to profile the pupil's performance, add up the number of correct answers the pupil has obtained in each strand and record these in the mark boxes on the front cover.

You can make a visual record of the pupil's progress by transferring the strand scores to the photocopiable Record Sheets, which take the form of a bar chart (pages 48–49). The national averages are shown in tints on each bar of the chart, so that you can compare the performance of a child or of the class against them.

Obtaining other scores

Refer to the appropriate tables in this manual to obtain the standardised score, age-standardised score, percentile, GPS age, Hodder Scale score and performance indicator for each pupil. You can then enter each pupil's scores on the photocopiable Record Sheets. Alternatively, use MARK to automate the whole score conversion process and to unlock *GaPS'* full performance analysis, diagnostic and predictive potential (see page 19).

In the tables beneath each term's mark scheme we have provided information about pupils' performance in *GaPS* from the standardisation trial. There is also a breakdown of the marks by strand. The mark schemes also include the facility for each question. This shows the percentage success on every question by pupils in the standardisation trial. All this information provides teachers with data to help them investigate a child's results.

In addition, the case studies in Chapter 4 show how teachers have been able to use this information along with standardised scores and the Hodder Scale to inform their teaching. Do be aware though that each of these measurement scales provides independent information and at times there will be differences between them, as they are generated using different methods. When they do give differing information this alerts teachers to investigate further, as it may be that a child has a patchy performance and that this is affecting the analyses.

The performance indicator bands reflect where children, groups, classes and the schools are in relation to other schools term on term. The termly tests sample a broad range of the National Curriculum content for that year, ensuring the child is assessed on an appropriate proportion of the curriculum content.

Using the online analysis and reports

MARK (My Assessment and Reporting Kit) is the powerful online platform that helps teachers to get more from *GaPS* and other assessments by RS Assessment from Hodder Education. To unlock your access to online analysis and reports within MARK go to www.risingstars-uk.com/mark. Detailed user guides and help to get started can be found online at www.rsassessment.com/support.

For customers using the paper tests you can record the marks that your pupils have scored in the *GaPS* tests. This can be done either by importing a CSV file containing their results, or by manually entering their scores via the marksheets.

On the 'Questions' tab you can view the facility value of each question and the average score across all the pupils who are in the class or group – allowing a quick onscreen view of which questions the class as a whole were doing well on or were struggling with.

On the 'Strands' tab, you can see the children's performance in each strand (grammar, punctuation, vocabulary and spelling), allowing a quick overview of how each child is performing by strand.

The Gap Analysis Export allows you to export a CSV with question level marks and a summary of performance at strand and test level.

You can generate a range of reports to analyse the performance of pupils, groups and classes.

- The individual pupil report shows the performance of an individual pupil on their most recently taken test.
- The pupil progress report compares the performance of an individual pupil across a number of tests.
- The intake, class or group report shows the performance of different groups on a specific test. There are three types of group report:
  - the progress report shows the performance of one group across a number of tests
  - the analysis report shows the performance of one group on a specific test, their average score and the national average standardised score
  - the listing report shows the performance of one group on a specific test, the proportion matching expectations and their average performance by strand.

Answers and mark scheme: *GaPS 1 Autumn*

Section A: Grammar, punctuation and vocabulary

Question	Answer and marking guidance	Strand reference	Facility %
1	Award **one mark** for: m ☑	V, G6 Letter (Reception)	86
2	Award **one mark** for: (sh)	V, G6 Letter (Reception)	87
3	Award **one mark** for: (my)	G, G3 G3.1 Sentences	78
4	Award **one mark** for: Can you see it? ☑	G, G2 G2.2 Questions	61
5	Award **one mark** for: (We went to the park.	P, G5 G5.1 Capital letters	64
6	Award **one mark** for: The (tent) is green.	G, G1 G1.1 Nouns	39
7	Award **one mark** for: (I) am riding my bike.	P, G5 G5.1 Capital letters	79
8	Award **one mark** if the words are in the correct order. Ignore minor copying errors. The cat sat on my lap. **Accept** letter reversal in spellings, i.e. reversed – s a u b d, etc.	G, G3 G3.1 Sentences	31
9	Award **one mark** for: The (black) dog sat by the fire.	G, G1 G1.3 Adjectives	34
10	Award **one mark** for: What is your name [?] **Accept** any recognisable question mark.	P, G5 G5.3 Question marks	36
11	Award **one mark** if the words are in the correct order. Ignore minor copying errors. The boy made a cake. **Accept** letter reversal in spellings, i.e. reversed – s a u b d, etc.	G, G3 G3.1 Sentences	41
12	Award **one mark** for: pool ☑	G, G1 G1.1 Nouns	66
13	Award **one mark** for: How fast can you run(?)	P, G5 G5.3 Question marks	87

Question	Answer and marking guidance	Strand reference	Facility %
14	Award **one mark** for: had ☑	V, G6 Words (Reception)	53
15	Award **one mark** if the words are in the correct order. Ignore minor copying errors. <u>The girl went for a swim.</u> **Accept** letter reversal in spellings, i.e. reversed – s a u b d, etc.	G, G3 G3.1 Sentences	26
16	Award **one mark** for: fluffy ☑	G, G1 G1.3 Adjectives	79
17	Award **one mark** for: My sister went to school. ☑	G, G3 G3.1 Sentences	61
18	Award **one mark** for: The (cold) milk was in the jug.	G, G1 G1.3 Adjectives	32
19	Award **one mark** for: The (moon) was silver.	G, G1 G1.1 Nouns	54
20	Award **one mark** if the words are in the correct order. Ignore minor copying errors. <u>An egg is in the cup.</u> **Accept** letter reversal in spellings, i.e. reversed – s a u b d, etc.	G, G3 G3.1 Sentences	22

Section B: Spelling

Question	Answer and marking guidance	Strand reference	Facility %
1	Award **one mark** for the correct spelling of the word **fish**.	Reception	79
2	Award **one mark** for the correct spelling of the word **coin**.	Reception	34
3	Award **one mark** for the correct spelling of the word **hand**.	Reception	71
4	Award **one mark** for: I took my coat **off**. The correct spelling of the word **off**.	S1 The sounds /f/, /l/, /s/, /z/ and /k/ spelled *ff*, *ll*, *ss*, *zz* and *ck*	30
5	Award **one mark** for: Your room is a **mess**. The correct spelling of the word **mess**.	S1 The sounds /f/, /l/, /s/, /z/ and /k/ spelled *ff*, *ll*, *ss*, *zz* and *ck*	22
6	Award **one mark** for: My boot **sank** into the mud. The correct spelling of the word **sank**.	S2 The /ŋ/ sound spelled *n* before *k* (e.g. *think*)	21
7	Award **one mark** for: They **have** gone swimming. The correct spelling of the word **have**.	S4 The /v/ sound at the end of words (e.g. *give*, *have*)	30
8	Award **one mark** for: We live in the same town as **my** grandad. The correct spelling of the word **my**.	S37 Common exception words	67

Question	Answer and marking guidance	Strand reference	Facility %
9	Award **one mark** for: I like **helping** my sister. The correct spelling of the word **helping**.	S6 Adding the endings –ing, –ed and –er to verbs where no change is needed in the root word (e.g. *hunting, hunted, hunter*)	32
10	Award **one mark** for: Sam got wet in the **rain**. The correct spelling of the word **rain**.	S8 Vowel digraphs and trigraphs: ai, ay, a–e (e.g. *rain, play, came*)	36
11	Award **one mark** for: I **was** playing with my toys. The correct spelling of the word **was**.	S37 Common exception words	53
12	Award **one mark** for: I can **see** a bus. The correct spelling of the word **see**.	S8 Vowel digraphs and trigraphs: ee	65
13	Award **one mark** for: The **boat** was on the pond. The correct spelling of the word **boat**.	S8 Vowel digraphs and trigraphs: oa	36
14	Award **one mark** for: There is a lion in the **zoo**. The correct spelling of the word **zoo**.	S8 Vowel digraphs and trigraphs: oo	71
15	Award **one mark** for: I want to **join** the game. The correct spelling of the word **join**.	S8 Vowel digraphs and trigraphs: oi	27
16	Award **one mark** for: The **clown** had a red nose. The correct spelling of the word **clown**.	S8 Vowel digraphs and trigraphs: ow	31
17	Award **one mark** for: We went shopping **today**. The correct spelling of the word **today**.	S37 Common exception words	37
18	Award **one mark** for: The teacher **said** we could read. The correct spelling of the word **said**.	S37 Common exception words	26
19	Award **one mark** for: Bella ate beef **pie**. The correct spelling of the word **pie**.	S8 Vowel digraphs and trigraphs: ie	14
20	Award **one mark** for: The man had a long **nose**. The correct spelling of the word **nose**.	S8 Vowel digraphs and trigraphs: ose	13

Answers and mark scheme: *GaPS 1 Autumn*

GaPS 1 Autumn: Analysis of performance by strand

Strand	Number of marks available	National average mark	National average %
Grammar	13	5.69	44
Punctuation	4	2.52	63
Vocabulary	3	2.19	73
Spelling	20	7.67	38
Total	40	18.06	45

Facility range and number of questions

Facility range	Number of questions at this facility
90–100%	0
60–89%	15
20–59%	23
0–19%	2

Answers and mark scheme: GaPS 1 Spring

Section A: Grammar, punctuation and vocabulary

Question	Answer and marking guidance	Strand reference	Facility %
1	Award **one mark** for: ⓦe went to the funfair.	P, G5 G5.1 Capital letters	84
2	Award **one mark** for: The ⓡats hid in the shed.	V, G6 G6.3 Suffixes	45
3	Award **one mark** for: ⓘn	G, G3 G3.1 Sentences	77
4	Award **one mark** for: What is the time? ☑	G, G2 G2.2 Questions	78
5	Award **one mark** for **both** correct. Ⓣheo and Ⓘ went to the field.	P, G5 G5.1 Capital letters	77
6	Award **one mark** for: The ⓓogs ran around the field.	V, G6 G6.3 Suffixes	51
7	Award **one mark** for: ⓐnd	G, G3 G3.3 Co-ordinating conjunctions	75
8	Award **one mark** for: What a lovely day it is⊙	P, G5 G5.4 Exclamation marks	94
9	Award **one mark** for: The clown had a ⓒurly beard.	G, G1 G1.3 Adjectives	46
10	Award **one mark** for: Where are my shoes ?_	P, G5 G5.3 Question marks	49
11	Award **one mark** for: <u>The bird sat in the tree.</u> Accept minor copying errors.	G, G3 G3.1 Sentences	65
12	Award **one mark** for **both** correct. Ⓘ went to see my friend Ⓜilo.	P, G5 G5.1 Capital letters	78
13	Award **one mark** for: Maisie cleaned her room ⓐnd made her bed.	V, Words (Reception)	34
14	Award **one mark** for: spiky ☑	G, G1 G1.3 Adjectives	65

Question	Answer and marking guidance	Strand reference	Facility %
15	Award **one mark** for: What game shall we play? Accept minor copying errors.	G, G3 G3.1 Sentences	35
16	Award **one mark** for: The rabbit has big ears. ☑	G, G3 G3.1 Sentences	77
17	Award **one mark** for: Jade (is brushing) her teeth.	G, G1 G1.2 Verbs	62
18	Award **one mark** for: The town had lots of (churches.)	V, G6 G6.3 Suffixes	57
19	Award **one mark** for: The (river) was fast.	G, G1 G1.1 Nouns	51
20	Award **one mark** for: The sky was dark and the stars were out. **Also accept:** The stars were out and the sky was dark. **Accept** minor copying errors.	G, G3 G3.1 Sentences	16

Section B: Spelling

Question	Answer and marking guidance	Strand reference	Facility %
1	Award **one mark** for: I **love** to sing. The correct spelling of the word **love**.	S37 Common exception words	67
2	Award **one mark** for: She has a cut on her **arm**. The correct spelling of the word **arm**.	S8 Vowel digraphs and trigraphs: ar	57
3	Award **one mark** for: They **played** tennis. The correct spelling of the word **played**.	S6 Adding the endings –ing, –ed and –er to verbs where no change is needed in the root word (*e.g. hunting, hunted, hunter*)	32
4	Award **one mark** for: There are **some** sheep in the field. The correct spelling of the word **some**.	S37 Common exception words	46
5	Award **one mark** for: He gave **her** a book. The correct spelling of the word **her**.	S8 Vowel digraphs and trigraphs: er	63
6	Award **one mark** for: My **skin** felt smooth. The correct spelling of the word **skin**.	S11 Using *k* for the /k/ sound (*e.g. kit, skin*)	37

Question	Answer and marking guidance	Strand reference	Facility %
7	Award **one mark** for: The **bird** was in the cage. The correct spelling of the word **bird**.	S8 Vowel digraphs and trigraphs: ir	52
8	Award **one mark** for: They sold candy floss at the **fair**. The correct spelling of the word **fair**.	S8 Vowel digraphs and trigraphs: air	34
9	Award **one mark** for: There is **one** muffin left. The correct spelling of the word **one**.	S37 Common exception words	69
10	Award **one mark** for: We **helped** tidy the classroom. The correct spelling of the word **helped**.	S6 Adding the endings –ing, –ed and –er to verbs where no change is needed in the root word (e.g. *hunting, hunted, hunter*)	27
11	Award **one mark** for: I cuddle my **bear** at bedtime. The correct spelling of the word **bear**.	S8 Vowel digraphs and trigraphs: ear	22
12	Award **one mark** for: The children went to a **party**. The correct spelling of the word **party**.	S9 Words ending in y (e.g. *very, funny*)	36
13	Award **one mark** for: Jack had very **short** trousers. The correct spelling of the word **short**.	S8 Vowel digraphs and trigraphs: or	52
14	Award **one mark** for: We can **hear** the wind. The correct spelling of the word **hear**.	S8 Vowel digraphs and trigraphs: ear	31
15	Award **one mark** for: I **saw** the kite. The correct spelling of the word **saw**.	S8 Vowel digraphs and trigraphs: aw	33
16	Award **one mark** for: The dog sleeps **when** he is tired. The correct spelling of the word **when**.	S37 Common exception words	39
17	Award **one mark** for: I have only been to the seaside **once**. The correct spelling of the word **once**.	S37 Common exception words	19
18	Award **one mark** for: I will **care** for my rabbit. The correct spelling of the word **care**.	S8 Vowel digraphs and trigraphs: are	18
19	Award **one mark** for: I can **come** to the cinema. The correct spelling of the word **come**.	S37 Common exception words	45
20	Award **one mark** for: In **August** we go on holiday. The correct spelling of the word **August**. **August** must be spelled with a capital A for the mark to be awarded.	S8 Vowel digraphs and trigraphs: au	15

GaPS 1 Spring: Analysis of performance by strand

Strand	Number of marks available	National average mark	National average %
Grammar	11	6.36	58
Punctuation	5	3.77	75
Vocabulary	4	1.81	45
Spelling	20	7.81	39
Total	40	19.75	49

Facility range and number of questions

Facility range	Number of questions at this facility
90–100%	1
60–89%	13
20–59%	22
0–19%	4

Answers and mark scheme: *GaPS 1 Summer*

Section A: Grammar, punctuation and vocabulary

Question	Answer and marking guidance	Strand reference	Facility %
1	Award **one mark** for: I help to tidy up. Ignore minor copying errors.	P, G5 G5.2 Full stops	63
2	Award **one mark** for: How are you feeling today ☑	G, G2 G2.2 Questions	81
3	Award **one mark** for: Today I was the special help<u>er</u>.	V, G6 G6.3 Suffixes	75
4	Award **one mark** for: Hamid and I went to the park to play football. Ignore minor copying errors.	P, G5 G5.1 Capital letters	41
5	Award **one mark** for: (ed)	V, G6 G6.3 Suffixes	66
6	Award **one mark** for: What a wet day it is(!)	P, G5 G5.4 Exclamation marks	93
7	Award **one mark** for: ing ☑	V, G6 G6.3 Suffixes	84
8	Award **one mark** for **both** correct. The (black) bird dropped the (sharp) stick.	G, G1 G1.3 Adjectives	46
9	Award **one mark** for: Can I have the milk ☑	P, G5 G5.3 Question marks	61
10	Award **one mark** for: Johnny was (running) to school. Also accept was running.	G, G1 G1.2 Verbs	69
11	Award **one mark** if the words are in the correct order. Our holiday started at the airport. Ignore minor copying errors.	G, G3 G3.1 Sentences	35
12	Award **one mark** for all **three** correct. (O)ur parents took (C)lodagh, (S)iobhan and me to the café.	P, G5 G5.1 Capital letters	71

Question	Answer and marking guidance	Strand reference	Facility %
13	Award **one mark** if the words are in the correct order. How many cakes are there? Ignore minor copying errors.	G, G2 G2.2 Questions	57
14	Award **one mark** for: Jamie brushed his teeth (and) got into bed.	G, G3 G3.3 Co-ordinating conjunctions	38
15	Award **one mark** for: long ☑	G, G1 G1.3 Adjectives	84
16	Award **one mark** for **both** correct. I put the (jam) in the (fridge).	G, G1 G1.1 Nouns	63
17	Award **one mark** if the words are in the correct order. I helped to pack away the toys. Ignore minor copying errors.	G, G3 G3.1 Sentences	55
18	Award **one mark** for: a verb ☑	G, G1 G1.2 Verbs	46
19	Award **one mark** for: The dog is brown and white. ☑	G, G3 G3.1 Sentences	87
20	Award **one mark** if the words are in the correct order. The sun was hot and the boys were swimming. **Also accept** The boys were swimming and the sun was hot. Ignore minor copying errors.	G, G3 G3.1 Sentences	32

Section B: Spelling

Question	Answer and marking guidance	Strand reference	Facility %
1	Award **one mark** for: I read the **book**. The correct spelling of the word **book**.	S8 Vowel digraphs and trigraphs: oo	71
2	Award **one mark** for: I can **pull** the rope. The correct spelling of the word **pull**.	S37 Common exception words	49
3	Award **one mark** for: The **wheel** kept spinning. The correct spelling of the word **wheel**.	S10 New consonant spellings *ph* and *wh*	24
4	Award **one mark** for: The **dolphin** swam in the sea. The correct spelling of the word **dolphin**.	S10 New consonant spellings *ph* and *wh*	26

Question	Answer and marking guidance	Strand reference	Facility %
5	Award **one mark** for: The **birds** were singing in the trees. The correct spelling of the word **birds**.	S5 Adding –s and –es to words (plural of nouns and the third-person singular of verbs)	56
6	Award **one mark** for: Tim **washes** his face. The correct spelling of the word **washes**.	S5 Adding –s and –es to words (plural of nouns and the third-person singular of verbs)	27
7	Award **one mark** for: The **bread** had cheese on top. The correct spelling of the word **bread**.	S8 Vowel digraphs and trigraphs: ea	32
8	Award **one mark** for: My coat is over **there**. The correct spelling of the word **there**.	S37 Common exception words	54
9	Award **one mark** for: **Friday** is my favourite day. The correct spelling of the word **Friday**. Friday must be spelled with a capital letter to award the mark.	S13 The days of the week	65
10	Award **one mark** for: The chickens were in the **farmyard**. The correct spelling of the word **farmyard**.	S12 Compound words	54
11	Award **one mark** for: We ate **blackberry** and apple crumble. The correct spelling of the word **blackberry**.	S12 Compound words	20
12	Award **one mark** for: My mum watched the **football**. The correct spelling of the word **football**.	S12 Compound words	48
13	Award **one mark** for: We played tag in the **playground**. The correct spelling of the word **playground**.	S12 Compound words	41
14	Award **one mark** for: My **friend** is going to the circus with me. The correct spelling of the word **friend**.	S37 Common exception words	25
15	Award **one mark** for: The woodlouse lives **under** the stone. The correct spelling of the word **under**.	S8 Vowel digraphs and trigraphs: er	66

Question	Answer and marking guidance	Strand reference	Facility %
16	Award **one mark** for: I **put** my bag by the door. The correct spelling of the word **put**.	S37 Common exception words	74
17	Award **one mark** for: Jane can **push** the swing. The correct spelling of the word **push**.	S37 Common exception words	68
18	Award **one mark** for: I take my lunch box to **school**. The correct spelling of the word **school**.	S37 Common exception words	50
19	Award **one mark** for: The **house** was on top of the hill. The correct spelling of the word **house**.	S37 Common exception words	49
20	Award **one mark** for: My bowl is **full** of cereal. The correct spelling of the word **full**.	S37 Common exception words	52

GaPS 1 Summer: Analysis of performance by strand

Strand	Number of marks available	National average mark	National average %
Grammar	12	6.83	57
Punctuation	5	3.26	65
Vocabulary	3	2.23	74
Spelling	20	9.39	47
Total	40	21.72	54

Facility range and number of questions

Facility range	Number of questions at this facility
90–100%	1
60–89%	16
20–59%	23
0–19%	0

Answers and mark scheme: GaPS 2 Autumn

Section A: Grammar, punctuation and vocabulary

Question	Answer and marking guidance	Strand reference	Facility %
1	Award **one mark** for: The dog buried his bone. Punctuation must be accurate to be awarded the mark. All listed words must be used for the mark to be awarded. **Also accept:** His dog buried the bone. Sentences which have additional words but with the meaning staying the same. e.g. *The black dog buried his juicy bone.* Ignore minor copying errors. **Do not accept:** Sentences which change the type of sentence. e.g. *Did the dog bury his bone?* Sentences which alter the content/focus. e.g. *The dog ate his bone.* When one of the listed words is missing. e.g. *the* or *his*	G, G3 G3.1 Sentences	38
2	Award **one mark** for: blue ☑	G, G1 G1.3 Adjectives	51
3	Award **one mark** for: Ask the lady for some cherries ☑	G, G2 G2.3 Commands	43
4	Award **one mark** for: ? ☑	P, G5 G5.3 Question marks	59
5	Award **one mark** for: statement ☑	G, G2 G2.1 Statements	39
6	Award **one mark** for: Stir the mixture very carefully — Adi ☑	G, G2 G2.3 Commands	56

Question	Answer and marking guidance	Strand reference	Facility %
7	Award **one mark** for: The classroom is messy (and) the children are noisy.	G, G3 G3.3 Co-ordinating conjunctions	43
8	Award **one mark** for: Tim made a chocolate cake. ☑	G, G4 G4.1a Simple past and simple present	56
9	Award one **mark** for **two** correct responses. | Noun	Singular	Plural
---	---	---
cats		✓
bag	✓	
pencils		✓		V, G6 G6.3 Suffixes	58
10	Award **one mark** for **two** correctly punctuated sentences, including full stops and capital letters. Nisha loves to play tennis. **S**he has lessons every weekend. **Accept** fully punctuated printed text as well as re-written, punctuated sentences.	P, G5 G5.2 Full stops (G, G3.1 Sentences; P, G5.1 Capital letters)	44
11	Award **one mark** for **all three** lines correctly drawn. tooth — fly gold — brush straw — berry butter — fish	V, G6 G6 Vocabulary	67
12	Award **one mark** for **two** correctly ticked boxes: beautiful flower ☑ old cottage ☑	G, G3 G3.2 Noun phrases	28
13	Award **one mark** for: What a fantastic party it was !	P, G5 G5.4 Exclamation marks	51

Question	Answer and marking guidance	Strand reference	Facility %
14	Award **one mark** for: What a beautiful flower that is — ! Put that in the rubbish bin — . Do you enjoy swimming — ? Your painting is fantastic — . **OR** What a beautiful flower that is — ! Put that in the rubbish bin — . Do you enjoy swimming — ? Your painting is fantastic — .	P, G5 G5 Punctuation	63
15	Award **one mark** for: Sam's socks are really smel<u>ly</u>.	V, G6 G6.3 Suffixes	46
16	Award **one mark** for: Kate has an <u>older brother called Ben</u>. ☑	G, G3 G3.2 Noun phrases	38
17	Award **one mark** for all **three** words circled. (every) (saturday) (i) go to my swimming lesson.	P, G5 G5.1 Capital letters	27
18	Award **one mark** for: The black and white dog barks loudly. ☑	G, G3 G3.1 Sentences	37
19	Award **one mark** for: I did my homework then watched television. ☑	G, G4 G4.2 Tense consistency	35
20	Award **one mark** for **all four** correct. Eat your dinner slowly . We had fish and chips for tea . Have you finished your dinner ? What a delicious meal that was !	P, G5 G5 Punctuation	16

Section B: Spelling

Question	Answer and marking guidance	Strand reference	Facility %
1	Award **one mark** for: The cup is **very** full. The correct spelling of the word **very**.	S9 Words ending –y (e.g. *very, funny*) (Year 1)	57
2	Award **one mark** for: Rama can **catch** a ball. The correct spelling of the word **catch**.	S3 –*tch* (Year 1)	39
3	Award **one mark** for: I **think** my school is great. The correct spelling of the word **think**.	S2 The /ŋ/ sound spelled *n* before *k*	53
4	Award **one mark** for: It is **cold** when it snows. The correct spelling of the word **cold**.	S37 Common exception words	67
5	Award **one mark** for: Our paintings were left to **dry**. The correct spelling of the word **dry**.	S22 The /aɪ/ sound spelled –*y* at the end of words	38
6	Award **one mark** for: It is very **kind** to share our toys. The correct spelling of the word **kind**.	S37 Common exception words	46
7	Award **one mark** for: Water can turn into **ice**. The correct spelling of the word **ice**.	S15 The /s/ sound spelled *c* before *e*, *i* and *y*	62
8	Award **one mark** for: The **babies** made lots of noise. The correct spelling of the word **babies**.	S23 Adding –*es* to nouns and verbs ending in –*y*	17
9	Award **one mark** for: Jack was **kicking** the ball into the goal. The correct spelling of the word **kicking**.	S6 Adding the endings –*ing*, –*ed* and –*er*	23
10	Award **one mark** for: Sam **fixed** his broken model. The correct spelling of the word **fixed**.	S6, S26 Adding the ending –*ed* (the exception that *x* is never doubled)	30
11	Award **one mark** for: Josh won the skipping **race**. The correct spelling of the word **race**.	S15 The /s/ sound spelled *c* before *e*, *i* and *y*	47

Question	Answer and marking guidance	Strand reference	Facility %
12	Award **one mark** for: Simon **wanted** to write a story. The correct spelling of the word **wanted**.	S6 Adding the endings –ing, –ed and –er	45
13	Award **one mark** for: Sarah loves to do **magic** tricks. The correct spelling of the word **magic**.	S14 The /dʒ/ sound spelled as –ge and –dge at the end of words, and sometimes spelled as g elsewhere in words before e, i and y	44
14	Award **one mark** for: Every **child** should be kept safe. The correct spelling of the word **child**.	S37 Common exception words	52
15	Award **one mark** for: My teacher was **talking** about healthy food. The correct spelling of the word **talking**.	S6 Adding the endings –ing, –ed and –er	32
16	Award **one mark** for: I love to read **fiction** books. The correct spelling of the word **fiction**.	S35 Words ending in –tion	13
17	Award **one mark** for: The school bell rang earlier than **usual**. The correct spelling of the word **usual**.	S33 The /ʒ/ sound spelled s	3
18	Award **one mark** for: Class two designed a **bridge**. The correct spelling of the word **bridge**.	S14 The /dʒ/ sound spelled as –ge and –dge	21
19	Award **one mark** for: Setsuko **dropped** her seeds into the pot. The correct spelling of the word **dropped**.	S26 Add –ing, –ed, –er, –est and –y to words of one syllable ending in a single consonant letter after a single vowel letter	9
20	Award **one mark** for: Ali put his **clothes** in the suitcase. The correct spelling of the word **clothes**.	S37 Common exception words	20

GaPS 2 Autumn: Analysis of performance by strand

Strand	Number of marks available	National average mark	National average %
Grammar	11	4.44	40
Punctuation	6	2.46	41
Vocabulary	3	1.62	54
Spelling	20	7.02	35
Total	40	15.54	39

Facility range and number of questions

Facility range	Number of questions at this facility
90–100%	0
60–89%	4
20–59%	31
0–19%	5

Answers and mark scheme: GaPS 2 Spring

Section A: Grammar, punctuation and vocabulary

Question	Answer and marking guidance	Strand reference	Facility %
1	Award **one mark** for: Did you clean your teeth this morning **?**	P, G5 G5.3 Question marks	68
2	Award **one mark** for: How many people came ☑	P, G5 G5.3 Question marks	75
3	Award **one mark** for: I was late for school the car broke down. (arrow/tick under "the")	G, G3 G3.4 Subordinating conjunctions	87
4	Award **one mark** for: Seb wanted to listen to his new CD (and) it did not work.	G, G3 G3.3 Co-ordinating conjunctions	74
5	Award **one mark** for: Jam sandwiches are my favourite — statement	G, G2 G2.1 Statements	54
6	Award **one mark** for: Drink your glass of water ☑ (Ali)	G, G2 G2.3 Commands	77
7	Award **one mark** for: The children couldn't go outside. ☑	P, G5 G5.8 Apostrophes	63
8	Award **one mark** for: (or)	G, G3 G3.3 Co-ordinating conjunctions	82

Question	Answer and marking guidance	Strand reference	Facility %
9	Award **one mark** for: if ☑	G, G3 G3.3 Co-ordinating conjunctions, G3.4 Subordinating conjunctions	56
10	Award **one mark** for: To make pancakes, you need flour, eggs, and milk	P, G5 G5.5 Commas in lists	64
11	Award **one mark** for: What a brilliant concert that was! The singers were my favourite.	P, G5 G5.4 Exclamation marks	41
12	Award **one mark** for: There was a brown, grizzly bare /(bear) in the woods.	V, G6 G6.5 Homophones and near-homophones	78
13	Award **one mark** for: Have you got a green ☑	G, G2 G2.2 Questions	54
14	Award one mark for: Megan finished her dinner then (has) a bath.	G, G4 G4.2 Tense consistency	43
15	Award **one mark** for: The bird sang (softly) in the tree.	G, G1 G1.6 Adverbs	72
16	Award **one mark** for **both** correct. David can shout loud**er** than me. Sophie can shout the loud**est**.	V, G6 G6.3 Suffixes	72
17	Award **one mark** for: Aziz is playing cricket. ☑	G, G4 G4.1d Present and past progressive	65
18	Award **one mark** for all **four** correct. 	Sentence	Statement	Command	 	---	---	---	 	Put your clothes in the wash basket.		✓	 	You will get dirty if you play in the mud.	✓		 	The garden is very muddy.	✓		 	Look at the mud on your clothes.		✓		G, G2 G2.1 Statements, G2.2 Commands	40

Question	Answer and marking guidance	Strand reference	Facility %
19	Award **one mark** for **all** correct. When I go **to** the safari park in **two** days, you can come **too**.	V, G6 G6.5 Homophones and near-homophones	53
20	Award **one mark** for: Look at the colourful rainbow. The sentence **must** be accurately punctuated. **Accept** minor copying errors.	G, G2 G2.3 Commands	39

Section B: Spelling

Question	Answer and marking guidance	Strand reference	Facility %
1	Award **one mark** for: I like to **jog** around the football field. The correct spelling of the word **jog**.	S14 The /dʒ/ sound spelled –ge and –dge at the end of words, and sometimes spelled g elsewhere in words before e, i and y (Autumn revision)	79
2	Award **one mark** for: Chen kicked the **ball**. The correct spelling of the word **ball**.	S27 The /ɔː/ sound spelled a before l and ll	79
3	Award **one mark** for: Seb unlocked the door with a **key**. The correct spelling of the word **key**.	S29 The /iː/ sound spelled –ey	79
4	Award **one mark** for: Polly played with her toy **cars**. The correct spelling of the word **cars**.	S5 Adding –s and –es to words (plurals of nouns and the third-person singular of verbs)	76
5	Award **one mark** for: We should not **talk** to strangers. The correct spelling of the word **talk**.	S27 The /ɔː/ sound spelled a before l and ll	79
6	Award **one mark** for: New York is an amazing **city**. The correct spelling of the word **city**.	S15 The /s/ sound spelled c before e, i and y (Autumn revision)	57
7	Award **one mark** for: Ben's teacher is called **Mrs** Smith. The correct spelling of the word **Mrs**. **Mrs** must be spelled with a capital **M** for the mark to be awarded.	S37 Common exception words	64

Question	Answer and marking guidance	Strand reference	Facility %
8	Award **one mark** for: The aeroplane flew in the sky **above** us. The correct spelling of the word **above**.	S28 The /ʌ/ sound spelled o	43
9	Award **one mark** for: Nisha fell and hurt her leg **badly**. The correct spelling of the word **badly**.	S34 The suffixes –ment, –ness, –ful, –less and –ly	39
10	Award **one mark** for: Lions live in the **wild**. The correct spelling of the word **wild**.	S37 Common exception words (Autumn revision)	65
11	Award **one mark** for: We go back to school on a **Monday**. The correct spelling of the word **Monday**. **Monday** must be spelled with a capital **M** for the mark to be awarded.	S28 The /ʌ/ sound spelled o	65
12	Award **one mark** for: The seed **hasn't** started to grow. The correct spelling of the word **hasn't**. **Hasn't** must be written as a single word without a space between **has** and **n't** for the mark to be awarded. The **apostrophe** must be clearly marked between the **n** and the **t** for the mark to be awarded.	S37 Common exception words	70
13	Award **one mark** for: The train stopped at the **station**. The correct spelling of the word **station**.	S37 Common exception words (Autumn revision)	35
14	Award **one mark** for: A postman **carries** his letters in a bag. The correct spelling of the word **carries**.	S23 Adding –es to nouns and verbs ending in y	20
15	Award **one mark** for: Jemal helped his dad do the **shopping**. The correct spelling of the word **shopping**.	S26 Adding –ing, –ed, –er, –est and –y to words of one syllable ending in a single consonant letter after a single vowel letter	17
16	Award **one mark** for: Kate got wet **because** it was raining. The correct spelling of the word **because**.	S37 Common exception words	37
17	Award **one mark** for: Marcus painted a **pretty** flower. The correct spelling of the word **pretty**.	S37 Common exception words	68

Question	Answer and marking guidance	Strand reference	Facility %
18	Award **one mark** for: Wissam put his <u>glove</u> in his pocket. The correct spelling of the word **glove**.	S28 The /ʌ/ sound spelled o	37
19	Award **one mark** for: A square <u>always</u> has four edges. The correct spelling of the word **always**.	S27 The /ɔ:/ sound spelled a before l and ll	46
20	Award **one mark** for: Cinderella lived <u>happily</u> ever after. The correct spelling of the word **happily**.	S34 The suffixes –ment, –ness, –ful, –less and –ly	32

GaPS 2 Spring: Analysis of performance by strand

Strand	Number of marks available	National average mark	National average %
Grammar	12	7.35	61
Punctuation	5	3.08	62
Vocabulary	3	2.00	67
Spelling	20	10.23	51
Total	40	22.66	57

Facility range and number of questions

Facility range	Number of questions at this facility
90–100%	0
60–89%	22
20–59%	17
0–19%	1

Answers and mark scheme: GaPS 2 Summer

Section A: Grammar, punctuation and vocabulary

Question	Answer and marking guidance	Strand reference	Facility %
1	Award **one mark** for: statement ☑	G, G2 G2.1 Statements	76
2	Award **one mark** for: What ☑	G, G2 G2.2 Questions	95
3	Award **one mark** for all **three** correct. I love to go swimming. It keeps me fit. It is also fun.	P, G5 G5.2 Full stops	84
4	Award **one mark** for: command ☑	G, G2 G2.3 Commands	89
5	Award **one mark** for **both** homophones correctly circled. I am number (one) / won. I one / (won) the trophy.	V, G6 G6.5 Homophones and near-homophones	80
6	Award **one mark** for: (Whos) going to take the dogs for a walk in the woods?	P, G5 G5.8 Apostrophes	55
7	Award **one mark** for: adjective ☑	G, G1 G1.3 Adjectives	73
8	Award **one mark** for: or (but) so and	G, G3 G3.3 Co-ordinating conjunctions	77
9	Award **one mark** for: What a clever puppy you are! ☑	P, G5 G5.4 Exclamation marks	71
10	Award **one mark** for: I went outside with my sister and I <u>play</u> football. ↑ played	G, G4 G4.2 Tense consistency	83

Question	Answer and marking guidance	Strand reference	Facility %
11	Award **one mark** for: When you went on holiday did you go to the beach I love the sand (tick shown under the space after "holiday")	P, G5 G5.3 Question marks	61
12	Award **one mark** for all ticks correct. | Sentence	Past tense	Present tense
---	---	---
Jemal sat on the chair.	✓	
Grandad drives the car.		✓
Tim walks to school.		✓
Polly made a drink.	✓			G, G4 G4.1a Simple past and simple present	49
13	Award **one mark** for **both** sentences correct. | Jenny hopped on one leg.	→	Jenny <u>was hopping</u> on one leg.
---	---	---
Tim blew the candles out.	→	Tim <u>was **blowing**</u> the candles out.
The choir sang a song.	→	The choir <u>was **singing**</u> a song.	 **Accept** spellings that are phonetically plausible.	G, G4 G4.1d Tense consistency	66
14	Award **one mark** for: tallest ☑	V, G6 G6.3 Suffixes	86
15	Award **one mark** for: At the zoo Helen saw a giraffe a lion and a tiger. (tick shown after "giraffe")	P, G5 G5.5 Commas in lists	69

44 Answers and mark scheme: *GaPS 2 Summer*

Question	Answer and marking guidance	Strand reference	Facility %
16	Award **one mark** for **both** correct. The River Thames is very **long**. The River Amazon is much **long(er)/ est**. The River Nile is the **long er /(est)**.	V, G6 G6.3 Suffixes	65
17	Award **one mark** for all **three** correct. (dry) ✓ (green) ✓ (scaly) ✓	G, G1 G1.3 Adjectives	60
18	Award **one mark** for **both** correct. slow ✓ sad ✓	G, G1 G1.6 Adverbs	68
19	Award **one mark** for all **three** correct. <u>They're</u> hanging <u>their</u> coats over <u>there</u> by the door.	V, G6 G6.5 Homophones and near-homophones	32
20	Award **one mark** for: Can you play the piano? Ignore minor copying errors.	G, G2 G2.1 Statements, G2.2 Questions	47

Section B: Spelling

Question	Answer and marking guidance	Strand reference	Facility %
1	Award **one mark** for: Jake's new kitten is really <u>small</u>. The correct spelling of the word **small**.	S27 The /ɔː/ sound spelled a before *l* and *ll*	84
2	Award **one mark** for: I can watch the film if <u>I'm</u> good. The correct spelling of the word **I'm**. **I'm** must be spelled with a capital **I** for the mark to be awarded.	S37 Common exception words	77
3	Award **one mark** for: George has a <u>bath</u> every night. The correct spelling of the word **bath**.	S37 Common exception words	85
4	Award **one mark** for: Some animals live in <u>bushes</u>. The correct spelling of the word **bushes**.	S5 Adding –s and –es to words (plurals of nouns and the third-person)	62

Answers and mark scheme: *GaPS 2 Summer*

Section B: Spelling

Question	Answer and marking guidance	Strand reference	Facility %
5	Award **one mark** for: Hassan is saving his pocket **money**. The correct spelling of the word **money**.	S29 The /i:/ sound spelled –ey	72
6	Award **one mark** for: An **apple** fell from the tree. The correct spelling of the word **apple**.	S18 The /l/ or /əl/ sound spelled –le at the end of words	67
7	Award **one mark** for: Nisha tried hard to finish her **work**. The correct spelling of the word **work**.	S31 The /ɜ:/ sound spelled or after w	72
8	Award **one mark** for: Ben dropped his **pencil** on the floor. The correct spelling of the word **pencil**.	S21 Words ending in –il	51
9	Award **one mark** for: A young **donkey** is called a foal. The correct spelling of the word **donkey**.	S29 The /i:/ sound spelled –ey	62
10	Award **one mark** for: All children need to **know** how to read. The correct spelling of the word **know**.	S16 The /n/ sound spelled kn– and (less often) gn– at the beginning of words	62
11	Award **one mark** for: Anna sat by the fire to keep **warm**. The correct spelling of the word **warm**.	S32 The /ɔ:/ sound spelled ar after w	67
12	Award **one mark** for: We **should** be kind to animals. The correct spelling of the word **should**.	S37 Common exception words	67
13	Award **one mark** for: Megan pulled a **petal** off the flower. The correct spelling of the word **petal**.	S20 The /l/ or /əl/ sound spelled –al at the end of words	35
14	Award **one mark** for: Joe felt full of **sadness**. The correct spelling of the word **sadness**.	S34 The suffixes –ment, –ness, –ful and –ly	67
15	Award **one mark** for: It is polite to **knock** on the door. The correct spelling of the word **knock**.	S16 The /n/ sound spelled kn– and (less often) gn– at the beginning of words	39
16	Award **one mark** for: Tom used his **towel** to dry himself. The correct spelling of the word **towel**.	S19 The /l/ or /əl/ sound spelled –el at the end of words	45

Question	Answer and marking guidance	Strand reference	Facility %
17	Award **one mark** for: Emma wandered round the **beautiful** garden. The correct spelling of the word **beautiful**.	S37 Common exception words	38
18	Award **one mark** for: Hundreds of **people** watched the football match. The correct spelling of the word **people**.	S37 Common exception words	66
19	Award **one mark** for: Mina's party was filled with **enjoyment**. The correct spelling of the word **enjoyment**.	S34 The suffixes –ment, –ness, –ful and –ly	54
20	Award **one mark** for: Robert loves to **write** stories. The correct spelling of the word **write**.	S17 The /r/ sound spelled wr at the beginning of words	57

GaPS 2 Summer: Analysis of performance by strand

Strand	Number of marks available	National average mark	National average %
Grammar	11	7.73	70
Punctuation	5	3.36	67
Vocabulary	4	2.60	65
Spelling	20	12.24	61
Total	40	25.93	65

Facility range and number of questions

Facility range	Number of questions at this facility
90–100%	1
60–89%	28
20–59%	11
0–19%	0

gaps Record Sheet
Pupil name ....

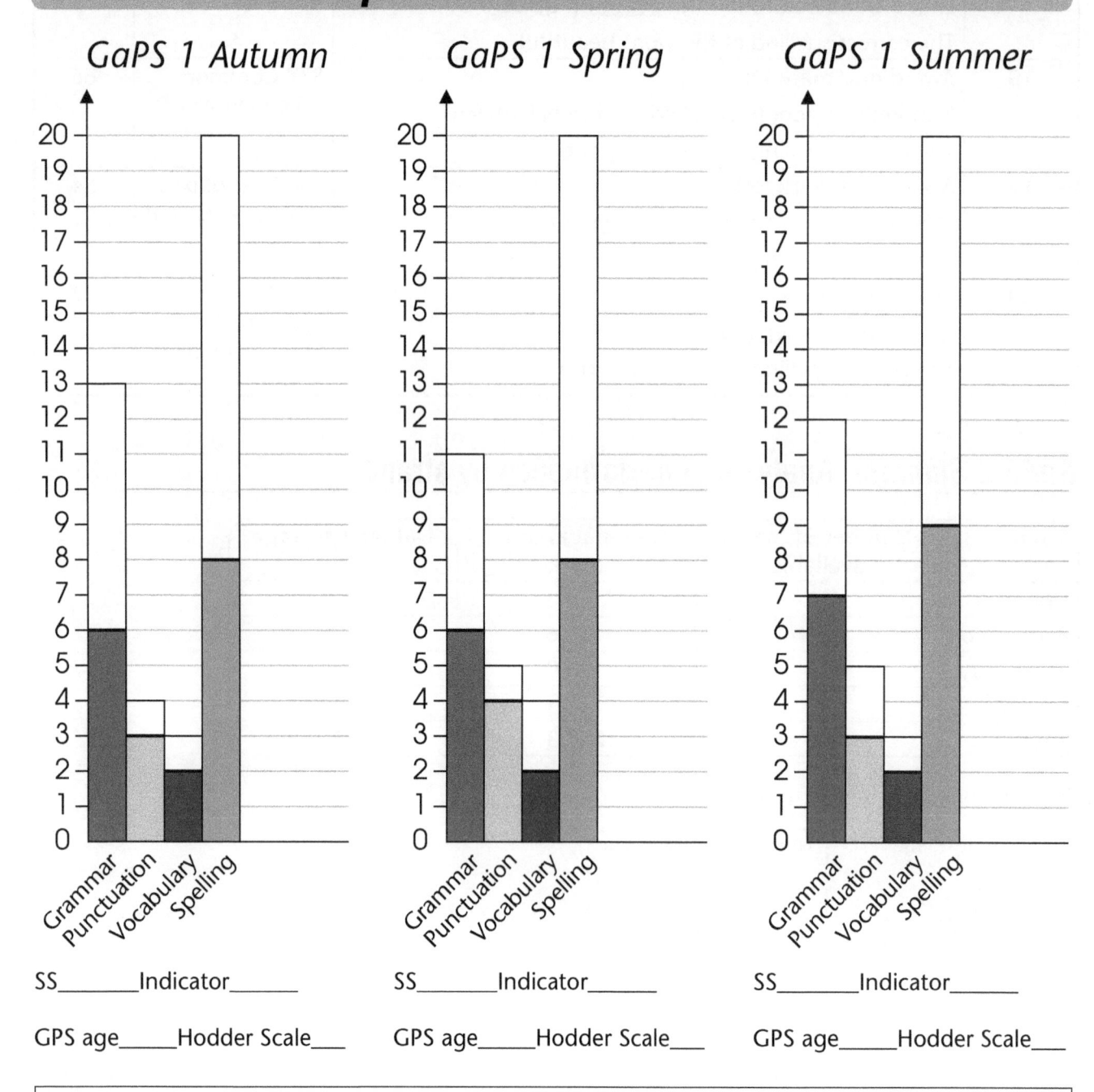

GaPS 1 Autumn

	Grammar	Punctuation	Vocabulary	Spelling
Pupil	6	3	2	8
Average	13	4	3	20

SS_____Indicator_____

GPS age_____Hodder Scale___

GaPS 1 Spring

	Grammar	Punctuation	Vocabulary	Spelling
Pupil	6	4	2	8
Average	11	5	4	20

SS_____Indicator_____

GPS age_____Hodder Scale___

GaPS 1 Summer

	Grammar	Punctuation	Vocabulary	Spelling
Pupil	7	3	2	9
Average	12	5	3	20

SS_____Indicator_____

GPS age_____Hodder Scale___

Note: The tints show the national average scores obtained in the standardisation trial rounded to whole marks.

© Rising Stars UK Ltd 2018. You may photocopy this page.

Record Sheet

gaps Record Sheet
Pupil name ....

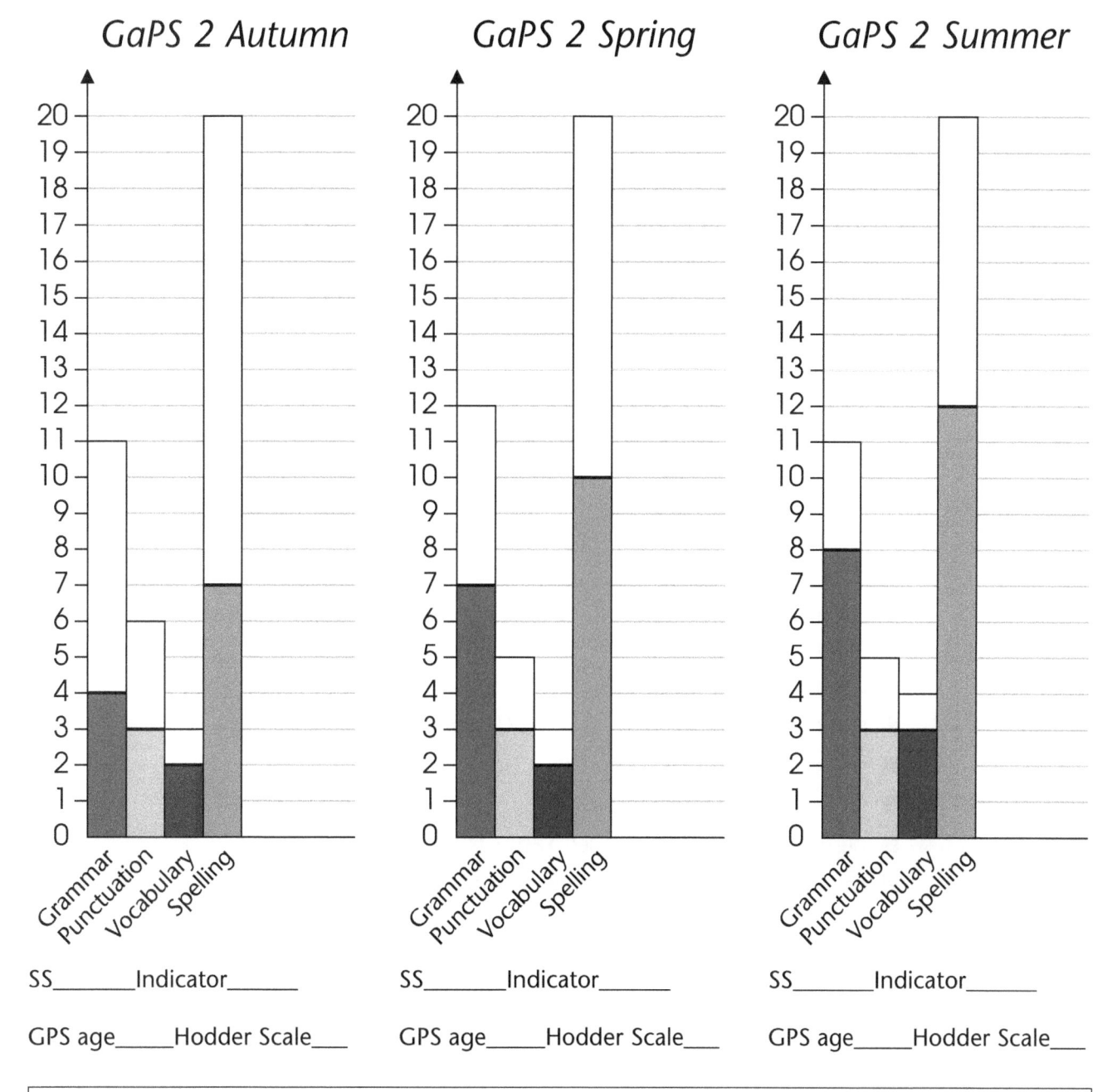

GaPS 2 Autumn

(Bar chart with y-axis 0–20; bars for Grammar: 11, Punctuation: 6, Vocabulary: 3, Spelling: 20. National average tints: Grammar 4, Punctuation 3, Vocabulary 2, Spelling 7.)

SS_____Indicator_____

GPS age_____Hodder Scale___

GaPS 2 Spring

(Bar chart with y-axis 0–20; bars for Grammar: 12, Punctuation: 5, Vocabulary: 3, Spelling: 20. National average tints: Grammar 7, Punctuation 3, Vocabulary 2, Spelling 10.)

SS_____Indicator_____

GPS age_____Hodder Scale___

GaPS 2 Summer

(Bar chart with y-axis 0–20; bars for Grammar: 11, Punctuation: 5, Vocabulary: 4, Spelling: 20. National average tints: Grammar 8, Punctuation 3, Vocabulary 3, Spelling 12.)

SS_____Indicator_____

GPS age_____Hodder Scale___

Note: The tints show the national average scores obtained in the standardisation trial rounded to whole marks.

© Rising Stars UK Ltd 2018. You may photocopy this page.

4 Test scores

Summative measures

Raw scores

A pupil's raw score is the total mark on a particular test. As an overview, you can evaluate how well a pupil has done by comparing his/her raw score to Table 4.1. This shows average raw scores from our national representative sample for each *GaPS* test by term and gender. You may also compare your class average raw scores to these averages, as shown in the tables beneath each term's mark scheme.

Table 4.1: Average raw scores for each test by term and gender in the standardisation trial

	Autumn test			*Spring test*			*Summer test*		
	Boys	Girls	Total	Boys	Girls	Total	Boys	Girls	Total
GaPS 1	16.2	18.9	18.1	18.3	20.3	19.8	20.1	22.7	21.7
GaPS 2	14.3	16.5	15.5	21.4	23.5	22.7	24.4	26.7	25.9

In addition to raw scores, the results obtained from *GaPS* will also enable you to report pupil performance in terms of:

- age-standardised score (see tables in **Chapter 6**);
- standardised score (see tables in **Chapter 6**);
- percentile (**Table 4.3** on page 53);
- GPS age (**Table 4.4** on page 54);
- performance indicators (see **Table 1.2** on page 8);
- the Hodder Scale; see **Table 4.5** on page 57).

Age-standardised scores, standardised scores and confidence bands

Both types of standardised score obtained from *GaPS* are standardised to a mean score of 100, immediately showing whether a pupil is above or below average as compared to the *GaPS* national standardisation sample. Age-standardised scores can be used to compare how a child is performing against other children of the same age (in months) from the cohort taking the same test. For example, a child who has a *standardised score* of 100 (i.e. who is at the mean average score of the whole cohort that took the test, including both older and younger children), could have a higher *age-standardised score* of, say 110, if that child is above average for their particular age (or the converse).

Standardised scores can be used to compare how a child is performing against all other children taking the same test, that is with other children or schools doing the same test.

Please note that age-standardised and standardised scores are quite different measures and are calculated differently. Therefore it is not appropriate to relate a child's age-standardised score to their standardised score.

Age-standardised scores

There are a number of advantages of using age-standardised scores for comparing summative performance. These include the following:

- They are standardised to an average score of 100, immediately showing whether a pupil is above or below average, relative to the *GaPS'* national standardisation sample.
- They allow comparisons to take into account the pupils' ages: pupils born earlier in the academic year are likely to have higher *raw scores* than younger pupils, but could have a lower *age-standardised score*. This enables you to rank pupils in order of achievement after age has been accounted for. *Note:* With older pupils, exposure to teaching is likely to have a significant if not greater impact on achievement than the chronological age of the child.

By definition, age-standardised scores suggest that older children will do better than younger children. In most tests, that span a number of years, this is indeed the case as age and experience do matter. However, the *GaPS* tests are written for each individual year group and our research found that in some tests age correlated weakly with performance, particularly in the Spring term tests. This is not surprising as the children were all receiving a fairly common experience based on national guidelines. This common experience tended to outweigh the effect of chronological age and we found that progress was weakly linked to age and reflects much more the quality of teaching.

The age-standardised scores provided in Chapter 6 range between 70 and 130, with a mean of 100 and a standard deviation (SD) of 15. The SD tells you how spread out the scores are from the mean.

Using the SD and the 'normal distribution' of scores, pupils can be grouped by performance into bands. Figure 4.1 below illustrates this grouping:

- Average refers to those whose performance is within one SD either side of the mean, i.e. 85–115.
- Below average and above average refer to those who are between one and two SDs either side of the mean, i.e. 70–85 and 115–130.

For many teachers, the term *average*, based on one SD each side of the mean, is too wide and so they prefer the *higher average* and *lower average* bands that are also shown on Figure 4.1 below and in Table 4.2 on page 52.

Figure 4.1: The normal distribution curve showing standard deviations, standardised and age-standardised scores, and percentiles

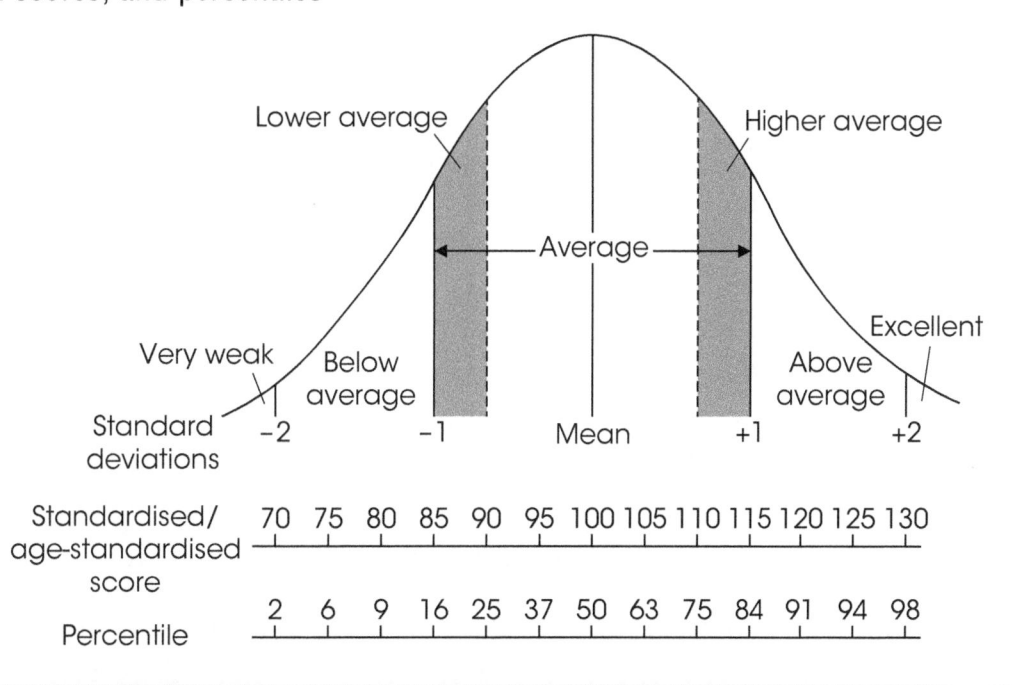

The 90 per cent confidence band for the Key Stage 1 *GaPS* tests is typically plus or minus 4 (see Table 5.2 on pages 61–62) – so for a pupil with an age-standardised score of, for example, 106 you can be 90 per cent confident that their 'true' score is between 102 and 110. This spread is lower than for many tests and indicative of the high reliability of the *GaPS* tests. To obtain an age-standardised score, first calculate the pupil's chronological age in years and completed months and then refer to the conversion tables in Chapter 6. Record this on the front of the test booklet.

Standardised scores

Standardised scores also have a norm (mean) of 100 and a standard deviation of 15, and in many ways are similar to age-standardised scores, except no allowance is made for the age of the child. As such, much of the above information applies to standardised scores.

We have included, in Chapter 6, standardised scores for all the *GaPS* tests. They are useful for comparing children from one cohort to another but require that the children take the same test for this comparison to be made. Look-up tables provided are based on the performance of the nationally representative sample. A score of 100 is an average score, whichever test the pupil uses. If a pupil gets a standardised score of 100 in Year 2 and they make average progress over the following year, we would also expect them to get a score of 100 in Year 3. If they get higher than 100 they will have made greater than expected progress, compared to our standardisation sample.

Table 4.2: Relationship between age-standardised/standardised test scores and qualitative interpretations

Standardised score	Qualitative interpretation	Standard deviation from mean	Percentile score	Percentage of normal population
>130	Excellent	>+2	>98	2.27
116–130	Above average	+1 to +2	84–98	13.59
110–115　　85–115　　85–90	Higher average　Average/age-appropriate　Lower average	–1 to +1	16–83	68.26
70–84	Below average	–1 to –2	2–15	13.59
<69	Very weak	<–2	<2	2.27

To suggest that one pupil is better than another and to place pupils in order of merit, you must be confident that the score obtained on the test is a reliable score and therefore a true reflection of ability. A 100% reliable score is always unknown because no test can be constructed to provide a perfect reflection of a person's ability. Therefore, tests often use confidence bands for each score to tell you how confident you can be that the score is a true score.

Percentiles

Percentiles can help to give you a better feel for the significance of a pupil's performance, because they show the percentage in each age group who score below a certain level. So an age-standardised or standardised score at the 68th percentile means that 68 per cent of the group scored below that pupil's standardised score. Thus the pupil is in the top third for his/her age group. Percentile scores may be derived from age-standardised scores or raw scores or anything else. To obtain a pupil's percentile, first calculate the pupil's chronological age in years and completed months, obtain his/

her age-standardised score using the appropriate conversion table at the end of this manual, and then refer to Table 4.3 below. Equally, standardised scores may be used in the same way but obviously without the need to reference a chronological age. The relationship between standardised or age-standardised scores and percentiles is most easily seen by reference to Figure 4.1 on page 51.

Table 4.3: Conversion of standardised and age-standardised scores to percentiles

Age-standardised score/ Standardised score	Percentile	Age-standardised score/ Standardised score	Percentile	Age-standardised score/ Standardised score	Percentile
≥130	≥98	108	70	89	24
128–9	97	107	68	88	22
126–7	96	106	66	87	20
125	95	105	63	86	18
123–4	94	104	60	85	16
122	93	103	58	84	14
121	92	102	55	83	13
120	91	101	52	82	12
119	90	100	50	81	11
118	89	99	48	80	9
117	87	98	45	79	8
116	86	97	42	78	7
115	84	96	40	76–7	6
114	82	95	37	75	5
113	80	94	34	73–4	4
112	78	93	32	71–2	3
111	77	92	30	70	2
110	74	91	28	<70	1
109	72	90	26		

Grammar, punctuation, vocabulary and spelling ages

Grammar, punctuation, vocabulary and spelling (GPS) ages can be used by teachers as a quick reference: a GPS age shows the *average* chronological age of the pupils who obtained each particular raw score – that is, the chronological age at which this level of performance is typical. However, for more detailed comparative information, and especially for tracking progress over time, age-standardised scores and percentiles are to be preferred.

Note that the GPS ages are provided for ages beyond the normal age range for a given year group. These have been generated by using statistical extrapolations, by up to six months either side of the main range of Key Stage 1 pupils taking the tests in the standardisation. Such extrapolations can be especially useful in interpreting the performance of weaker pupils who have been given a test for a younger age range. To obtain a pupil's GPS age, use Table 4.4 on page 54 and read across from the pupil's raw score to the appropriate column for the test taken. Record this on the front of the test booklet. Alternatively use the tables on page 63 onwards for quick reference.

Table 4.4: GPS ages for each term

Raw score	GaPS 1 Autumn	GaPS 1 Spring	GaPS 1 Summer	GaPS 2 Autumn	GaPS 2 Spring	GaPS 2 Summer	Raw score
1	<4:10	<5:0	<5:5	<5:6	<5:6	<5:8	1
2	<4:10	<5:0	<5:5	<5:6	<5:6	<5:8	2
3	<4:10	<5:0	<5:5	<5:6	<5:6	<5:8	3
4	<4:10	<5:0	<5:5	<5:6	<5:6	<5:8	4
5	<4:10	<5:0	<5:5	<5:6	<5:6	<5:8	5
6	<4:10	<5:0	<5:5	<5:6	<5:6	<5:8	6
7	<4:10	<5:0	<5:5	<5:6	<5:6	<5:8	7
8	<4:10	<5:0	<5:5	5:6	<5:6	<5:8	8
9	<4:10	<5:0	<5:5	5:7	<5:6	<5:8	9
10	4:10	5:0	<5:5	5:9	<5:6	<5:8	10
11	5:0	5:1	<5:5	5:10	<5:6	<5:8	11
12	5:1	5:2	<5:5	6:0	<5:6	<5:8	12
13	5:2	5:3	<5:5	6:1	<5:6	<5:8	13
14	5:3	5:4	<5:5	6:3	<5:6	<5:8	14
15	5:4	5:5	5:5	6:4	5:6	<5:8	15
16	5:5	5:7	5:6	6:5	5:8	5:8	16
17	5:7	5:8	5:7	6:7	5:10	5:9	17
18	5:8	5:9	5:8	6:8	6:0	5:11	18
19	5:9	5:10	5:9	6:10	6:1	6:0	19
20	5:10	5:11	5:10	6:11	6:3	6:1	20
21	5:11	6:0	5:11	7:1	6:5	6:3	21
22	6:0	6:1	6:0	7:2	6:7	6:4	22
23	6:2	6:2	6:1	7:4	6:9	6:6	23
24	6:3	6:4	6:2	7:5	6:11	6:7	24
25	6:4	6:5	6:3	7:7	7:1	6:9	25
26	6:5	6:6	6:4	7:8	7:2	6:10	26
27	6:6	6:7	6:5	7:9	7:4	6:11	27
28	6:7	6:8	6:7	7:11	7:6	7:1	28
29	6:9	6:9	6:8	8:0	7:8	7:2	29
30	6:10	6:10	6:9	8:2	7:10	7:4	30
31	6:11	6:11	6:10	8:3	8:0	7:5	31
32	7:0	7:1	6:11	8:5	8:1	7:6	32
33	7:1	7:2	7:0	>8:5	8:3	7:8	33
34	>7:1	7:3	7:1	>8:5	8:5	7:9	34
35	>7:1	7:4	7:2	>8:5	8:7	7:11	35
36	>7:1	7:5	7:3	>8:5	>8:7	8:0	36
37	>7:1	7:6	7:4	>8:5	>8:7	8:2	37
38	>7:1	>7:6	7:5	>8:5	>8:7	8:3	38
39	>7:1	>7:6	7:6	>8:5	>8:7	8:4	39
40	>7:1	>7:6	7:7	>8:5	>8:7	8:6	40

Hodder Scale scores

Refer to the table on page 57 to obtain the Hodder Scale score and predicted score for each pupil. This scale is provided as a decimal scale from 0–7 and allows you to monitor the pupils' progress. It is also useful if the pupil falls outside the chronological age range of the age-standardised score table for the test used, because you may still obtain a score on the Hodder Scale.

Diagnostic and formative interpretation

Summative measures are valuable to provide an *overall* picture of the child's performance relative to his/her peers. Such data may, for example, confirm that the pupil is doing well for his/her age and indicate that no intervention strategy is required. However, a more detailed check may show, for example, that good performance in one part of the test is masking poor performance on another area.

Use the *GaPS* profile to look for patterns of strengths and weaknesses

Use the *GaPS* profile on the Record Sheets (pages 48–49) or the version on MARK (the online analysis and reporting tool) to see if there are patterns of strengths and weaknesses in:

- Grammar
- Punctuation
- Vocabulary
- Spelling.

Every pupil has particular strengths and weaknesses that will show up in the *GaPS* profile. When you examine the pupil's answers, you can see when there is a change from correct to incorrect answers and at what level of demand this is occurring. This may alert you to generally weak achievement or perhaps to weakness (or strength) in one specific aspect of the curriculum. This may highlight aspects of grammar, punctuation, vocabulary or spelling which have previously been taught but which have been forgotten or were not understood at the time.

It should be borne in mind when undertaking this form of analysis that performance will naturally reflect recent teaching.

Check a pupil's performance on a specific question

You may also go one stage further and check a pupil's individual performance on a specific question and compare how they have performed relative to other pupils in the same year group. Refer to the mark scheme to see what proportion of pupils in that year group answered each question correctly. This is called the facility and is shown as a percentage: 60 per cent shows that 60 per cent of pupils in the nationally representative sample answered the question correctly. If you wish, you can also average your pupils' scores to create an overall *class* or *cohort* profile. The pattern revealed may inform both teaching and target setting, as it will highlight the areas in which pupils are secure or confident and those that need to be addressed.

Obtaining patterns and predictions of performance

The online analysis and reports will make it easier to automatically pinpoint areas of strength and weakness which is explained on page 19.

You are able to monitor progress in the strands and to track pupil progress term by term, plus it provides predictions of future performance and an opportunity to monitor against previous performance (see next section). Predictions of progress can also be obtained from the table on page 57.

The case studies later in this chapter indicate how this comparative information enables some next steps to be planned. With this more detailed picture, it is possible to implement specific teaching strategies to help both low and high attaining pupils to improve.

Reporting progress using the Hodder Scale

In developing the *GaPs* tests, six cohorts of pupils – totalling more than 6000 pupils – were tracked termly over a full academic year. Using this information it was possible to link pupil performance from term to term and year to year, to identify patterns that provide a firm basis on which to project future performance and establish realistic expectations.

The Hodder Scale score is a useful monitoring scale, as it shows a decimalised measure of progress and enables teachers to monitor progress term by term, enabling you to predict pupils' future performance and measure whether current progress is what would have been expected. The tables on pages 63–68 provide, for each test, a complete set of reference data for reporting progress in terms of the Hodder Scale score. Read across from the pupil's raw score on a particular test to the Hodder Scale score. Record this score on the front of the test booklet. This will give you the Hodder Scale score the pupil should achieve in any future term.

Predicting future performance with the Hodder Scale

You may wish to set targets for the future and monitor progress over a term or year. This is possible for both individual pupils and whole classes, by drawing on the average performance data of over 1000 pupils in each year group, from term to term and across all the years, in the standardisation sample. The table on page 57 provides this information.

In Key Stage 1, expected progress is roughly 0.3 Hodder Scale score every term. Some children do better than this, others less well. In Table 4.5 on page 57 look up the term in which the pupil took the test and follow across to see the predicted Hodder Scale score they should achieve if they follow the progress of an average pupil.

For example, a pupil who achieves a Hodder Scale score of 1.3 on the *GaPS 1 Autumn* test, and who makes average progress, might be expected to have a Hodder Scale score of 1.9 in the *GaPS 1 Summer* test, and 3.8 in the *GaPS 4 Summer* test – and ultimately to gain 2.8 at the end of Year 2. In practice, of course, no pupil is 'average' and progress is rarely completely smooth. In addition, the further ahead one is looking, the more tentative are the predictions one can make (see below). The Hodder Scale, however, does provide a well-founded empirically-based statistical basis for making predictions about performance which can then be modified in the light of actual progress.

Monitoring the difference between the *actual* Hodder Scale score and the *predicted* average Hodder Scale score – for an individual pupil or for a whole class – enables you to see if there is increasing divergence or convergence to normal progress.

Table 4.5: Monitoring and predicting progress on a term-by-term basis **from Year 1 through to Year 2**

This table has been conflated for easy use. If there is no Hodder Scale score for that term this is because this score does not relate to a mark in the test. For scores at the very top and bottom end use the detailed tables on page 63 onwards.

Average Hodder Scale score					
GaPS 1 Autumn	GaPS 1 Spring	GaPS 1 Summer	GaPS 2 Autumn	GaPS 2 Spring	GaPS 2 Summer
				1.3	1.5
				1.5	1.8
0.1	0.4	0.7	1.3	1.6	1.9
0.3	0.6	0.9	1.3	1.6	1.9
0.5	0.7	1.0	1.3	1.6	1.9
	0.8	1.1	1.4	1.7	2.0
0.6	0.9	1.2	1.5	1.8	2.1
0.7	1.0	1.3	1.6	1.9	2.2
0.8	1.1	1.4	1.7	2.0	2.3
0.9	1.2	1.5	1.8	2.1	2.4
1.0	1.3	1.6	1.9	2.2	2.5
1.1	1.4	1.7	2.0	2.3	2.6
1.2	1.5	1.8	2.1	2.4	2.7
1.3	1.6	1.9	2.2	2.5	2.8
1.4	1.7	2.0	2.3	2.6	2.9
1.5	1.8	2.1	2.4	2.7	3.0
1.6	1.9	2.2	2.5	2.8	3.1
1.7	2.0	2.3	2.6	2.9	3.2
1.8	2.1	2.4	2.7	3.0	3.3
1.9	2.2	2.5	2.8	3.1	3.3
2.0	2.3	2.6	2.9	3.2	3.3
2.1	2.4	2.7	3.0	3.2	3.3
2.2	2.5	2.7	3.0	3.2	3.3
2.3	2.6	2.7	3.0	3.2	3.3
2.5	2.6	2.7	3.0	3.2	3.3
			3.1	3.2	3.3
			3.2	3.2	3.3

Case studies

Case study 1 – Chen (Year 2)

Chen is one of our Year 2 pupils. He joined our school in Reception with English as an additional language. Chen is a bright little boy and performed well above average in maths during Year 1. However, his performance on the *GaPS* tests in Year 1 showed that, after making a good start in the Autumn term, he was falling behind:

GaPS 1 Autumn		GaPS 1 Spring		GaPs 1 Summer	
Hodder Scale	Standardised score	Hodder Scale	Standardised score	Hodder Scale	Standardised score
1.3	102	1.4	92	1.6	90

Based on his performance in the *GaPS 1 Autumn* test Chen's teacher had expected Chen to reach 1.9 on the Hodder Scale in the Summer test with a standardised score of 100–102.

Looking at the graphs on Chen's Record Sheet it became clear that Chen was doing very well in the *GaPS* spelling test sections but that he was performing lower than expected on grammar questions. The spelling results were not a surprise as Chen had done very well in his phonics test at the end of Year 1.

As a result of this finding Chen was put into a small group with additional TA support at the start of Year 2 to specifically support him with English grammar. His *GaPS 2 Autumn* test showed improvements in performance on grammar questions as did his results on the *GaPS 2 Spring* test. We are now confident that Chen will meet at least the expected standard in his end of key stage test for grammar, punctuation and spelling.

Case study 2 – Sophie (Year 1)

Sophie is in Year 1. She left Reception having achieved a Good Level of Development (GLD) but her score in the *GaPS 1 Autumn* test was lower than expected. She only scored 12 marks out of 40 giving her a standardised score of 90. This surprised Sophie's teacher as in class Sophie was quick to put up her hand and generally answered questions correctly. Sophie's scores in maths tests were also lower than expected.

Sophie's teacher was concerned about her apparent underperformance and decided to review Sophie's test results in more detail. Using MARK she spotted that Sophie had no scores for questions at the end of the Section A (grammar, punctuation and vocabulary) part of the *GaPS* test and also no scores for some of the spellings in Section B. Checking back through the test paper showed that Sophie had not attempted those questions.

The teacher watched Sophie closely in class and noticed that she was slow at handwriting and was also not completing all her work. This was also observed for maths work and was clearly evident throughout Sophie's books for the term. It was clear that Sophie was underperforming because her motor skills needed further development and that she needed more support in holding and using a pencil as she was not doing this correctly. The teacher immediately put one-to-one support in place to address Sophie's handwriting issues and provided some practice materials for her to use at home. Improvements were seen very quickly in Sophie's books, and in the *GaPS 1 Spring* test she scored 19 out of 40 with a standardised score of 99 which was much closer to what her teacher expected. A review of her test papers and the data in MARK showed that Sophie had attempted all but the final two questions in the grammar, punctuation and vocabulary part of the test and all the spellings, so the interventions were proving effective.

Case study 3 – Abdul (Year 2)

Abdul is in Year 2. In the *GaPS* test in the Summer term at the end of Year 1 he scored 31 out of 40 and had a standardised score of 114 and a Hodder Scale score of 2.2. This was a pleasing result and supported his teacher's judgement that he was an above average child. When Abdul moved into Year 2 this was demonstrated further. In the *GaPS 2 Autumn* test he gained a raw score of 30, a standardised score of 124 and a Hodder Scale score of 2.7. This was considerably above the *GaPS* predicted Hodder score of 2.5 and suggested that Abdul had previously been underperforming.

Abdul's teacher reviewed his Record Sheet which showed that Abdul was doing particularly well on grammar questions. She wanted to ensure that Abdul was being fully stretched in class and so provided him with more opportunities to use his grammar skills to create more complex sentences in writing work. At the start of the Summer term Abdul is on track to get a high score in his end of Key Stage test and also to be judged as working at greater depth in his overall Key Stage 1 writing assessment.

5 Technical information

Standardisation sample

In order for us to have confidence in our statistical analyses it is vital that we have a large enough sample of pupils that sat each test. We aimed for a baseline of around 1000 completed scripts for each year group.

To account for some scripts not being returned or some schools dropping out of the trial we distributed 1500 scripts for each year group across 32 schools. This meant that each school received around 40 scripts on average for each year group.

When it came to return completed scripts there was some drop out, with most of the schools returning fewer scripts than had been sent to them. In most cases the final analysis included approximately 1000 scripts and we were therefore confident that the analyses provided reliable results. The fewest scripts we received and analysed was for the Year 2 test where we had 951 scripts which we deemed acceptable as being close to 1000.

We also looked at how representative the samples were of the population of KS2 pupils on two criteria: disadvantage and performance. This was done using the Edubase schools' database (https://get-information-schools.service.gov.uk/).

We looked at the proportion of disadvantaged pupils in each school which are defined as:

- Those who were eligible for free school meals in the last 6 years or are looked after by the LA for a day or more or who have been adopted from care.

The second criteria regarding the proportion of high performing pupils in the school is defined below:

- Those achieving level 5 or above in reading and maths tests at the end of Key Stage 2 and in writing teacher assessment.

From Edubase we calculated the national average proportion (at a school level) which gave us the proportion of disadvantaged pupils as 0.32 and the proportion of high performing pupils as 0.24.

We then compared our sample to the national average and found that the proportion of disadvantaged pupils was approximately the same (0.32) as the national average and the proportion of high performing pupils (0.23) was also approximately the same as the national average. This means that we are confident that the final sample is reasonably representative of the national population.

Reliability

The reliability of a test indicates whether or not we would get similar results from repeated administrations of the test with similar samples of pupils. An appropriate measure of test reliability for *GaPS* is Cronbach's alpha (α), which measures *internal consistency* reliability. To interpret the value of Cronbach's alpha (the reliability coefficient), rules of thumb are useful. Table 5.1 gives us some useful ranges used in practice.

Table 5.1: Rule of thumb for interpreting Cronbach's alpha values

Range of alpha values	Interpretation
$\alpha \geq 0.9$	Excellent
$0.8 \leq \alpha < 0.9$	Good
$0.7 \leq \alpha < 0.8$	Acceptable
$0.6 \leq \alpha < 0.7$	Questionable
$0.5 \leq \alpha < 0.6$	Poor
$\alpha < 0.5$	Unacceptable

The information for each test is given in Table 5.2 below and shows that the tests are extremely reliable.

All test scores are subject to some margin of error. This does not mean that a child has been assessed incorrectly, but rather that we are making a statistical estimate of the accuracy of the test as a measuring instrument. There are two ways of reporting this margin of error. One is the 90% (or 95%) confidence band and the other is the standard error of measurement (SEM). Using the confidence band, we can say that we are 90% confident that the child's 'true' scores lie in a certain range around the obtained score. The 90 per cent confidence band for Key Stage 1 *GaPS* age-standardised scores is +/–4, as shown in Table 5.2 below. This means, for example, that for a child 7:5 (seven years and five months) who obtains a raw score of 15 on the *GaPS 2 Autumn* test and hence a standardised score of 99, we can say with 90 per cent confidence that their 'true' standardised score lies between 95 and 103. The confidence band for each test is presented in Table 5.2 below. The SEM estimates how pupils' scores would be distributed around their true score if they took the test several times. The smaller the SEM the more reliable the score. The SEM for each test is also presented in Table 5.2.

For tests targeting a particular age range, we use a standardisation method based on *percentile norms* – the fundamental principle being that scores at the same percentile rank are comparable. Hence a pupil at, say, the 30th percentile in his/her age group has the same relative ability as a pupil at the 30th percentile in any other age group. The standardisation procedure that we have used for these tests is called the *non-parallel linear regression model*. It is the recognised method for age standardising educational tests.[1]

Table 5.2: Sample statistics and reliability measures

GaPS 1	Autumn 2016	Spring 2017	Summer 2017
Sample size for age-standardisation	827	984	789
Number of children	956	1128	1176
Number of boys	373	463	474
Number of girls	422	515	502
Mean mark	18.1	19.8	21.7
Boys mean mark	16.2	18.3	20.1
Girls mean mark	18.9	20.3	22.7
Cronbach Alpha	0.92	0.93	0.94
Pearson coefficient	0.87	0.92	0.84
90% confidence band for mean	(13.3, 22.9)	(15.0, 24.6)	(16.9, 26.5)
Standard Error of Measurement	2.94	2.89	2.89

---

[1] Our basic methodology follows D.G. Lewis (see *Statistical Methods in Education*, University of London Press, 1972, pp. 86–96), with enhancements outlined by I. Schagen (see 'A Method for the Age Standardisation of Test Scores', *Applied Psychological Measurement*, 14, 4, December 1990, pp. 387–93).

GaPS 2	Autumn 2016	Spring 2017	Summer 2017
Sample size for age-standardisation	733	774	617
Number of children	982	1027	951
Number of boys	384	417	373
Number of girls	409	441	425
Mean mark	15.5	22.7	25.9
Boys mean mark	14.3	21.4	24.4
Girls mean mark	16.5	23.5	26.7
Cronbach Alpha	0.94	0.95	0.95
Pearson coefficient	0.77	0.78	0.81
90% confidence band for mean	(10.1, 20.9)	(17.4, 28.0)	(20.8, 31.0)
Standard Error of Measurement	3.28	3.2	3.08

Validity

Strong *validity* for a test like *GaPS* means that the test addresses the material in the curriculum which the children have studied and been taught. Each test, from Year 1 to Year 6, was written to revise the content from the previous term and assess the content for the term the test is set for. This ensures that tests taken towards the end of the term are valid, however, the teacher should reassure themself that the content set out in the curriculum map for the term (and previous terms) has been covered. Additionally, the test itself must have high reliability (see pages 60–61) so that the results would be replicated by repeated administrations of the test.

6 Standardised score tables

Standardised scores, Hodder Scale scores and GPS ages for *GaPS*

The following tables include the standardised score, the Hodder Scale score, the predicted Hodder Scale score for the next term and the GPS age mapped to the raw score for each test.

GaPS 1 Autumn: Standardised scores, Hodder Scale scores and GPS ages

Raw score	Standardised score	Hodder Scale score	Predicted Hodder Scale score	GPS age
1	72	0.1	0.4	
2	74	0.3	0.6	
3	75	0.5	0.7	
4	77	0.6	0.9	
5	78	0.6	0.9	<4:10
6	80	0.7	1.0	
7	82	0.8	1.1	
8	83	0.8	1.1	
9	85	0.9	1.2	
10	87	0.9	1.2	4:10
11	88	1.0	1.3	5:0
12	90	1.0	1.3	5:1
13	92	1.1	1.4	5:2
14	93	1.1	1.4	5:3
15	95	1.2	1.5	5:4
16	97	1.2	1.5	5:5
17	98	1.2	1.5	5:7
18	100	1.3	1.6	5:8
19	102	1.3	1.6	5:9
20	103	1.4	1.7	5:10
21	105	1.4	1.7	5:11
22	107	1.4	1.7	6:0
23	108	1.5	1.8	6:2
24	110	1.5	1.8	6:3
25	111	1.6	1.9	6:4
26	113	1.6	1.9	6:5
27	115	1.6	1.9	6:6
28	116	1.7	2.0	6:7
29	118	1.7	2.0	6:9
30	120	1.8	2.1	6:10
31	121	1.8	2.1	6:11
32	123	1.9	2.2	7:0
33	125	1.9	2.2	7:1
34	126	2.0	2.3	
35	128	2.0	2.3	
36	130	2.1	2.4	
37	130	2.2	2.5	>7:1
38	130	2.3	2.6	
39	130	2.5	2.6	
40	130	2.5	2.6	

GaPS 1 Spring: Standardised scores, Hodder Scale scores and GPS ages

Raw score	Standardised score	Hodder Scale score	Predicted Hodder Scale score	GPS age
1	70	0.4	0.7	<5:0
2	72	0.4	0.7	
3	73	0.4	0.7	
4	75	0.6	0.9	
5	76	0.7	1.0	
6	78	0.8	1.1	
7	80	0.9	1.2	
8	81	1.0	1.3	
9	83	1.1	1.4	
10	84	1.1	1.4	5:0
11	86	1.2	1.5	5:1
12	88	1.2	1.5	5:2
13	89	1.3	1.6	5:3
14	91	1.3	1.6	5:4
15	92	1.4	1.7	5:5
16	94	1.4	1.7	5:7
17	96	1.5	1.8	5:8
18	97	1.5	1.8	5:9
19	99	1.5	1.8	5:10
20	100	1.6	1.9	5:11
21	102	1.6	1.9	6:0
22	104	1.7	2.0	6:1
23	105	1.7	2.0	6:2
24	107	1.7	2.0	6:4
25	108	1.8	2.1	6:5
26	110	1.8	2.1	6:6
27	112	1.8	2.1	6:7
28	113	1.9	2.2	6:8
29	115	1.9	2.2	6:9
30	116	2.0	2.3	6:10
31	118	2.0	2.3	6:11
32	120	2.1	2.4	7:1
33	121	2.1	2.4	7:2
34	123	2.1	2.4	7:3
35	124	2.2	2.5	7:4
36	126	2.3	2.6	7:5
37	128	2.3	2.6	7:6
38	129	2.4	2.7	>7:6
39	130	2.5	2.7	
40	130	2.6	2.7	

GaPS 1 Summer: Standardised scores, Hodder Scale scores and GPS ages

Raw score	Standardised score	Hodder Scale score	Predicted Hodder Scale score	GPS age
1	70	0.7	1.3	<5:5
2	70	0.7	1.3	<5:5
3	72	0.7	1.3	<5:5
4	73	0.7	1.3	<5:5
5	75	0.7	1.3	<5:5
6	76	0.9	1.3	<5:5
7	78	1.0	1.3	<5:5
8	79	1.1	1.4	<5:5
9	81	1.2	1.5	<5:5
10	82	1.3	1.6	<5:5
11	84	1.4	1.7	<5:5
12	85	1.4	1.7	<5:5
13	87	1.5	1.8	<5:5
14	88	1.5	1.8	<5:5
15	90	1.6	1.9	5:5
16	91	1.6	1.9	5:6
17	93	1.7	2.0	5:7
18	94	1.7	2.0	5:8
19	96	1.8	2.1	5:9
20	97	1.8	2.1	5:10
21	99	1.8	2.1	5:11
22	100	1.9	2.2	6:0
23	102	1.9	2.2	6:1
24	103	1.9	2.2	6:2
25	105	2.0	2.3	6:3
26	106	2.0	2.3	6:4
27	108	2.1	2.4	6:5
28	109	2.1	2.4	6:7
29	111	2.1	2.4	6:8
30	112	2.2	2.5	6:9
31	114	2.2	2.5	6:10
32	116	2.3	2.6	6:11
33	117	2.3	2.6	7:0
34	119	2.3	2.6	7:1
35	120	2.4	2.7	7:2
36	122	2.4	2.7	7:3
37	123	2.5	2.8	7:4
38	125	2.6	2.9	7:5
39	126	2.6	2.9	7:6
40	128	2.7	3.0	7:7

GaPS 2 Autumn: Standardised scores, Hodder Scale scores and GPS ages

Raw score	Standardised score	Hodder Scale score	Predicted Hodder Scale score	GPS age
1	76	1.3	1.6	<5:6
2	77	1.4	1.7	
3	79	1.5	1.8	
4	81	1.6	1.9	
5	82	1.7	2.0	
6	84	1.7	2.0	
7	86	1.8	2.1	
8	87	1.8	2.1	5:6
9	89	1.9	2.2	5:7
10	91	1.9	2.2	5:9
11	92	2.0	2.3	5:10
12	94	2.0	2.3	6:0
13	96	2.0	2.3	6:1
14	97	2.1	2.4	6:3
15	99	2.1	2.4	6:4
16	101	2.2	2.5	6:5
17	102	2.2	2.5	6:7
18	104	2.2	2.5	6:8
19	106	2.3	2.6	6:10
20	107	2.3	2.6	6:11
21	109	2.4	2.7	7:1
22	111	2.4	2.7	7:2
23	112	2.4	2.7	7:4
24	114	2.5	2.8	7:5
25	116	2.5	2.8	7:7
26	117	2.5	2.8	7:8
27	119	2.6	2.9	7:9
28	121	2.6	2.9	7:11
29	122	2.7	3.0	8:0
30	124	2.7	3.0	8:2
31	126	2.8	3.1	8:3
32	127	2.8	3.1	8:5
33	129	2.9	3.2	>8:5
34	130	3.0	3.2	
35	130	3.1	3.2	
36	130	3.2	3.2	
37	130	3.2	3.2	
38	130	3.2	3.2	
39	130	3.2	3.2	
40	130	3.2	3.2	

GaPS 2 Spring: Standardised scores, Hodder Scale scores and GPS ages

Raw score	Standardised score	Hodder Scale score	Predicted Hodder Scale score	GPS age
1	70	1.3	1.5	<5:6
2	70	1.3	1.5	
3	70	1.3	1.5	
4	70	1.3	1.5	
5	72	1.3	1.5	
6	74	1.3	1.5	
7	75	1.5	1.8	
8	77	1.6	1.9	
9	78	1.7	2.0	
10	80	1.8	2.1	
11	82	1.9	2.2	
12	83	1.9	2.2	
13	85	2.0	2.3	
14	86	2.1	2.4	
15	88	2.1	2.4	5:6
16	89	2.2	2.5	5:8
17	91	2.2	2.5	5:10
18	93	2.2	2.5	6:0
19	94	2.3	2.6	6:1
20	96	2.3	2.6	6:3
21	97	2.4	2.7	6:5
22	99	2.4	2.7	6:7
23	101	2.4	2.7	6:9
24	102	2.5	2.8	6:11
25	104	2.5	2.8	7:1
26	105	2.6	2.9	7:2
27	107	2.6	2.9	7:4
28	108	2.6	2.9	7:6
29	110	2.7	3.0	7:8
30	112	2.7	3.0	7:10
31	113	2.8	3.1	8:0
32	115	2.8	3.1	8:1
33	116	2.8	3.1	8:3
34	118	2.9	3.2	8:5
35	120	2.9	3.2	8:7
36	121	3.0	3.3	>8:7
37	123	3.0	3.3	
38	124	3.1	3.3	
39	126	3.1	3.3	
40	127	3.2	3.3	

GaPS 2 Summer: Standardised scores, Hodder Scale scores and GPS ages

Raw score	Standardised score	Hodder Scale score	Predicted Hodder Scale score	GPS age
1	70	1.5	1.8	<5:8
2	70	1.5	1.8	
3	70	1.5	1.8	
4	70	1.5	1.8	
5	70	1.5	1.8	
6	70	1.5	1.8	
7	70	1.5	1.8	
8	72	1.5	1.8	
9	73	1.5	1.8	
10	75	1.8	2.0	
11	77	1.9	2.2	
12	78	2.0	2.3	
13	80	2.1	2.4	
14	81	2.2	2.5	
15	83	2.2	2.5	
16	84	2.3	2.6	5:8
17	86	2.3	2.6	5:9
18	88	2.4	2.7	5:11
19	89	2.4	2.7	6:0
20	91	2.5	2.8	6:1
21	92	2.5	2.8	6:3
22	94	2.6	2.9	6:4
23	95	2.6	2.9	6:6
24	97	2.6	2.9	6:7
25	99	2.7	3.0	6:9
26	100	2.7	3.0	6:10
27	102	2.8	3.1	6:11
28	103	2.8	3.1	7:1
29	105	2.8	3.1	7:2
30	106	2.9	3.2	7:4
31	108	2.9	3.2	7:5
32	110	3.0	3.3	7:6
33	111	3.0	3.3	7:8
34	113	3.0	3.3	7:9
35	114	3.1	3.4	7:11
36	116	3.1	3.4	8:0
37	117	3.2	3.5	8:2
38	119	3.2	3.5	8:3
39	121	3.2	3.5	8:4
40	122	3.3	3.6	8:6

Age-standardised scores

GaPS 1 Autumn: Age-standardised scores

Raw score	5:1	5:2	5:3	5:4	5:5	5:6	5:7	5:8	5:9	5:10	5:11	6:0	6:1	6:2	Raw score
1					Award 69 for all scores in this area										1
2	71	70													2
3	76	74	73	72	71	71	70								3
4	80	79	77	76	75	74	73	72	71	70					4
5	84	82	81	80	78	77	76	75	74	73	72	71	70		5
6	87	85	84	83	82	80	79	78	76	75	74	73	72	71	6
7	89	88	87	85	84	83	82	80	79	78	76	75	74	73	7
8	91	90	89	88	87	85	84	83	81	80	79	77	76	75	8
9	93	92	91	89	88	87	86	85	83	82	81	80	78	77	9
10	96	94	93	91	90	89	88	87	85	84	83	82	80	79	10
11	98	96	95	93	92	91	89	88	87	86	85	83	82	81	11
12	100	98	97	96	94	92	91	90	89	88	87	85	84	83	12
13	101	100	99	97	96	94	93	91	90	89	88	87	86	84	13
14	102	101	100	99	98	96	95	93	92	91	89	88	87	86	14
15	103	102	101	100	99	98	97	95	94	92	91	90	89	88	15
16	105	104	102	101	100	99	98	97	95	94	92	91	90	89	16
17	107	105	104	103	101	101	100	98	97	96	94	92	91	90	17
18	108	107	106	104	103	102	101	100	99	97	96	94	93	91	18
19	110	108	107	106	104	103	102	101	100	99	97	96	95	93	19
20	111	110	108	107	106	104	103	102	101	100	99	98	96	95	20
21	113	112	110	109	107	106	105	103	102	101	100	99	98	96	21
22	114	113	112	110	109	107	106	105	103	102	101	100	99	98	22
23	116	115	113	112	110	109	108	106	105	104	102	101	100	99	23
24	118	116	115	114	112	111	109	108	107	105	104	102	101	101	24
25	119	118	116	115	114	112	111	109	108	107	106	104	103	102	25
26	121	120	118	117	115	114	113	111	110	108	107	106	104	103	26
27	122	121	120	119	117	116	114	113	112	110	109	107	106	105	27
28	123	122	121	120	119	118	116	115	113	112	111	109	108	106	28
29	125	124	123	122	121	120	118	117	115	114	113	111	110	108	29
30	127	125	124	123	122	121	120	119	117	116	114	113	112	110	30
31	129	128	126	125	124	123	122	121	120	118	117	115	114	113	31
32		130	129	127	126	124	123	122	121	120	119	118	116	115	32
33			130	129	127	126	124	123	122	121	120	119	117		33
34					130	129	127	126	124	123	122	121	120		34
35								129	128	126	125	124	123		35
36										130	129	128	126		36
37															37
38															38
39															39
40					Award 131 for all scores in this area										40
	5:1	5:2	5:3	5:4	5:5	5:6	5:7	5:8	5:9	5:10	5:11	6:0	6:1	6:2	

Raw score	Age in years and completed months											Raw score
	6:3	6:4	6:5	6:6	6:7	6:8	6:9	6:10	6:11	7:0	7:1	7:2	
1	Award 69 for all scores in this area												1
2													2
3													3
4													4
5													5
6	70												6
7	72	71	70	70									7
8	74	73	72	71	70								8
9	76	75	74	73	72	71	70						9
10	78	77	75	74	73	72	71	70	70				10
11	80	78	77	76	75	74	73	72	71	70			11
12	81	80	79	78	76	75	74	73	72	71	70		12
13	83	82	81	79	78	77	75	74	73	72	72	71	13
14	85	83	82	81	80	78	77	76	75	74	73	72	14
15	86	85	84	82	81	80	79	77	76	75	74	73	15
16	88	87	85	84	83	81	80	79	78	76	75	74	16
17	89	88	87	85	84	83	82	80	79	78	77	75	17
18	90	89	88	87	86	84	83	82	81	79	78	77	18
19	91	90	89	88	87	86	84	83	82	81	79	78	19
20	93	92	90	89	88	87	86	85	83	82	81	80	20
21	95	93	92	91	89	88	87	86	85	83	82	81	21
22	97	95	94	92	91	90	89	88	86	85	84	82	22
23	98	97	95	94	92	91	90	89	88	86	85	84	23
24	100	98	97	96	94	92	91	90	89	88	87	85	24
25	101	100	99	97	96	94	93	91	90	89	88	87	25
26	102	101	100	99	98	96	95	93	92	90	89	88	26
27	103	102	101	100	99	98	97	95	93	92	91	90	27
28	105	104	102	101	101	100	98	97	95	94	92	91	28
29	107	106	104	103	102	101	100	99	97	96	94	93	29
30	109	107	106	105	103	102	101	100	99	98	97	95	30
31	111	110	108	107	106	104	103	102	101	100	99	97	31
32	114	112	111	109	108	107	105	104	102	101	101	100	32
33	116	115	113	112	110	109	107	106	105	104	102	101	33
34	119	118	116	115	113	112	110	109	108	106	105	104	34
35	122	121	119	118	117	115	114	113	111	110	108	107	35
36	124	124	123	122	120	119	118	116	115	114	112	111	36
37	130	128	127	125	124	123	122	121	120	119	117	115	37
38					130	128	127	125	124	123	122		38
39													39
40	Award 131 for all scores in this area												40
	6:3	6:4	6:5	6:6	6:7	6:8	6:9	6:10	6:11	7:0	7:1	7:2	

GaPS 1 Autumn: Age-standardised scores

GaPS 1 Spring: Age-standardised scores

Raw score	5:5	5:6	5:7	5:8	5:9	5:10	5:11	6:0	6:1	6:2	6:3	6:4	6:5	6:6	Raw score
1					Award 69 for all scores in this area										1
2															2
3	74	73	72	71	70										3
4	78	77	76	75	73	72	71	70							4
5	82	80	79	78	77	75	74	73	72	71	70				5
6	84	83	82	81	79	78	77	76	74	73	72	71	70		6
7	87	86	84	83	82	81	79	78	77	76	74	73	72	71	7
8	89	88	87	85	84	83	82	80	79	78	76	75	74	73	8
9	91	90	89	87	86	85	83	82	81	80	78	77	76	75	9
10	93	92	91	89	88	87	85	84	83	82	80	79	78	77	10
11	95	94	92	91	90	88	87	86	84	83	82	81	79	78	11
12	97	95	94	93	91	90	89	87	86	85	84	82	81	80	12
13	98	97	96	95	93	92	90	89	88	86	85	84	83	81	13
14	100	99	97	96	95	93	92	91	89	88	87	85	84	83	14
15	101	100	99	97	96	95	94	92	91	90	88	87	86	84	15
16	103	101	100	99	98	96	95	94	92	91	90	88	87	86	16
17	104	103	101	100	99	98	96	95	94	92	91	90	88	87	17
18	105	104	103	102	100	99	98	96	95	94	92	91	90	89	18
19	107	105	104	103	102	100	99	98	96	95	94	92	91	90	19
20	108	107	105	104	103	102	100	99	98	96	95	94	93	91	20
21	110	108	107	105	104	103	102	100	99	98	97	95	94	93	21
22	111	110	108	107	105	104	103	102	100	99	98	97	95	94	22
23	112	111	110	109	107	106	104	103	102	100	99	98	97	95	23
24	114	112	111	110	109	107	106	105	103	102	101	99	98	97	24
25	115	114	112	111	110	109	107	106	105	103	102	101	99	98	25
26	117	116	114	113	112	111	109	107	106	105	104	102	101	100	26
27	119	117	116	114	113	112	111	109	108	106	105	104	103	101	27
28	120	119	118	116	115	113	112	111	110	108	107	105	104	103	28
29	121	120	119	118	117	115	114	112	111	110	109	107	106	104	29
30	123	122	121	120	118	117	116	114	113	112	111	109	108	106	30
31	124	123	122	121	120	119	118	116	115	113	112	111	110	108	31
32	126	124	124	123	122	121	120	118	117	116	114	113	112	111	32
33	129	127	125	124	123	122	121	120	119	118	117	115	114	112	33
34		130	129	127	125	124	123	122	121	120	119	118	117	115	34
35					129	127	126	124	123	123	122	121	120	118	35
36						130	129	127	125	124	123	122	121	36
37											129	127	126	124	37
38															38
39															39
40					Award 131 for all scores in this area										40
	5:5	5:6	5:7	5:8	5:9	5:10	5:11	6:0	6:1	6:2	6:3	6:4	6:5	6:6	

Raw score	6:7	6:8	6:9	6:10	6:11	7:0	7:1	7:2	7:3	7:4	7:5	7:6	Raw score
				Age in years and completed months									
1					Award 69 for all scores in this area								1
2													2
3													3
4													4
5													5
6													6
7	70												7
8	72	71	70										8
9	74	72	71	70									9
10	75	74	73	72	71	70							10
11	77	76	75	73	72	71	70						11
12	79	77	76	75	74	73	71	70					12
13	80	79	78	76	75	74	73	72	71	70			13
14	82	80	79	78	77	75	74	73	72	71	70		14
15	83	82	81	79	78	77	76	74	73	72	71	70	15
16	84	83	82	81	79	78	77	76	75	73	72	71	16
17	86	85	83	82	81	80	78	77	76	75	73	72	17
18	87	86	85	83	82	81	80	78	77	76	75	74	18
19	89	87	86	85	83	82	81	80	78	77	76	75	19
20	90	89	87	86	85	83	82	81	80	79	77	76	20
21	91	90	89	87	86	85	84	82	81	80	79	77	21
22	93	91	90	89	87	86	85	84	82	81	80	79	22
23	94	93	91	90	89	88	86	85	84	82	81	80	23
24	96	94	93	92	90	89	88	86	85	84	83	81	24
25	97	96	95	93	92	90	89	88	86	85	84	83	25
26	99	97	96	95	93	92	91	89	88	87	85	84	26
27	100	99	97	96	95	94	92	91	90	88	87	86	27
28	102	100	99	98	96	95	94	92	91	90	89	87	28
29	103	102	100	99	98	97	96	94	93	91	90	89	29
30	105	104	102	101	100	99	97	96	95	93	92	91	30
31	107	105	104	103	102	100	99	98	96	95	94	92	31
32	109	108	106	105	104	102	101	100	99	97	96	95	32
33	111	110	109	107	106	105	103	102	101	99	98	97	33
34	114	112	111	110	109	107	106	104	103	102	101	99	34
35	117	115	114	112	112	111	109	107	106	105	104	102	35
36	120	119	118	116	115	113	112	111	110	108	107	105	36
37	123	123	122	121	119	118	117	115	114	112	111	110	37
38	130	128	127	125	124	123	122	121	120	119	118	116	38
39									129	128	126	124	39
40				Award 131 for all scores in this area									40
	6:7	6:8	6:9	6:10	6:11	7:0	7:1	7:2	7:3	7:4	7:5	7:6	

GaPS 1 Spring: Age-standardised scores

GaPS 1 Summer: Age-standardised scores

Raw score	5:7	5:8	5:9	5:10	5:11	6:0	6:1	6:2	6:3	6:4	6:5	6:6	6:7	6:8	Raw score
1	Award 69 for all scores in this area													1
2															2
3	73	72	71	70											3
4	76	75	74	73	72	71	70	70							4
5	80	78	77	76	75	74	73	72	71	70	70				5
6	82	81	80	79	78	77	76	75	74	73	72	71	70		6
7	85	84	83	81	80	79	78	77	76	75	74	73	72	71	7
8	87	86	85	84	82	81	80	79	78	77	76	75	74	73	8
9	89	88	87	86	84	83	82	81	80	79	77	76	75	74	9
10	90	89	88	87	86	85	84	83	82	81	79	78	77	76	10
11	92	91	90	89	88	87	86	85	83	82	81	80	79	78	11
12	93	92	91	90	89	88	87	86	85	84	83	82	80	79	12
13	94	93	92	91	91	90	89	88	86	85	84	83	82	81	13
14	96	95	94	93	92	91	90	89	88	87	86	85	83	82	14
15	97	96	95	94	93	92	91	90	89	88	87	86	85	84	15
16	98	97	96	95	94	93	92	91	90	89	88	87	86	85	16
17	99	98	97	96	95	94	93	92	91	90	90	88	87	86	17
18	100	100	99	98	96	95	94	93	92	92	91	90	89	88	18
19	102	101	100	99	98	97	96	95	94	93	92	91	90	89	19
20	103	102	101	100	99	98	97	96	95	94	93	92	91	90	20
21	104	103	102	101	100	99	98	97	96	95	94	93	92	91	21
22	105	104	103	102	101	100	99	98	97	96	95	94	93	92	22
23	107	106	104	103	102	101	100	99	98	97	96	95	94	93	23
24	108	107	106	105	103	102	101	100	99	99	97	96	95	94	24
25	109	108	107	106	105	104	103	102	101	100	99	98	97	96	25
26	111	110	109	108	106	105	104	103	102	101	100	99	98	97	26
27	112	111	110	109	108	107	105	104	103	102	101	100	99	98	27
28	114	113	111	110	109	108	107	106	105	104	102	101	100	100	28
29	115	114	113	112	111	110	109	108	106	105	104	103	102	101	29
30	117	115	114	113	112	111	110	109	108	107	106	105	103	102	30
31	118	117	116	115	114	113	112	111	110	109	108	106	105	104	31
32	120	119	118	117	116	115	114	113	112	111	109	108	107	106	32
33	122	121	120	119	118	117	116	115	114	113	112	110	109	108	33
34	124	123	122	121	120	119	118	117	116	115	114	113	112	111	34
35	128	127	125	124	123	122	120	119	118	117	116	115	114	113	35
36			130	128	126	125	124	123	121	120	119	118	117	116	36
37						129	128	126	124	123	122	121	120	37
38												129	127	126	38
39															39
40	Award 131 for all scores in this area													40
	5:7	5:8	5:9	5:10	5:11	6:0	6:1	6:2	6:3	6:4	6:5	6:6	6:7	6:8	

Raw score	6:9	6:10	6:11	7:0	7:1	7:2	7:3	7:4	7:5	7:6	7:7	7:8	7:9	7:10	Raw score
					Age in years and completed months										
1					Award 69 for all scores in this area										1
2															2
3															3
4															4
5															5
6															6
7	70														7
8	72	71	70												8
9	73	72	71	71	70										9
10	75	74	73	72	71	70									10
11	76	75	74	73	72	72	71	70							11
12	78	77	76	75	74	73	72	71	70						12
13	80	78	77	76	75	74	73	72	71	70	70				13
14	81	80	79	78	77	75	74	73	73	72	71	70			14
15	83	81	80	79	78	77	76	75	74	73	72	71	70		15
16	84	83	82	81	79	78	77	76	75	74	73	72	71	70	16
17	85	84	83	82	81	80	78	77	76	75	74	73	72	71	17
18	87	85	84	83	82	81	80	79	77	76	75	74	73	72	18
19	88	87	86	84	83	82	81	80	79	78	77	75	74	73	19
20	89	88	87	86	85	84	82	81	80	79	78	77	76	75	20
21	90	89	88	87	86	85	84	83	81	80	79	78	77	76	21
22	91	90	89	88	87	86	85	84	83	82	80	79	78	77	22
23	92	91	90	89	88	87	86	85	84	83	82	81	80	78	23
24	93	92	91	91	90	89	88	86	85	84	83	82	81	80	24
25	95	94	93	92	91	90	89	88	87	86	84	83	82	81	25
26	96	95	94	93	92	91	90	89	88	87	86	85	84	83	26
27	97	96	95	94	93	92	91	90	89	88	87	86	85	84	27
28	99	98	96	95	94	93	92	92	91	90	89	88	87	85	28
29	100	99	98	97	96	95	94	93	92	91	90	89	88	87	29
30	101	100	99	98	97	96	95	94	93	92	91	91	90	89	30
31	103	102	101	100	99	98	97	96	95	94	93	92	91	90	31
32	105	104	103	102	101	100	99	98	97	96	95	94	93	92	32
33	107	106	105	104	103	101	101	100	99	98	97	96	95	94	33
34	109	108	107	106	105	104	103	102	101	100	99	98	97	96	34
35	112	111	110	109	108	107	105	104	103	102	101	100	99	98	35
36	115	114	113	112	111	110	109	108	106	105	104	103	102	101	36
37	119	118	117	116	115	114	113	112	110	109	108	107	106	105	37
38	124	123	122	121	120	119	118	117	116	115	114	113	112	110	38
39						130	128	126	124	123	122	121	120	119	39
40				Award 131 for all scores in this area										130	40
Raw score	6:9	6:10	6:11	7:0	7:1	7:2	7:3	7:4	7:5	7:6	7:7	7:8	7:9	7:10	Raw score

GaPS 1 Summer: Age-standardised scores

GaPS 2 Autumn: Age-standardised scores

Raw score	6:1	6:2	6:3	6:4	6:5	6:6	6:7	6:8	6:9	6:10	6:11	7:0	7:1	Raw score
1	Award 69 for all scores in this area													1
2	71	70	70											2
3	75	75	74	73	73	72	72	71	70	70				3
4	81	80	79	78	77	76	75	74	74	73	72	72	71	4
5	85	85	84	83	82	81	80	78	77	77	76	75	74	5
6	88	87	87	86	85	85	84	82	81	80	79	78	77	6
7	91	90	89	88	88	87	86	85	85	84	83	82	81	7
8	93	92	91	91	90	89	88	88	87	86	85	85	84	8
9	94	94	93	92	92	91	90	90	89	88	87	87	86	9
10	96	95	94	94	93	93	92	91	91	90	89	88	88	10
11	97	96	96	95	95	94	93	93	92	92	91	90	90	11
12	98	98	97	96	96	95	95	94	94	93	92	92	91	12
13	100	99	99	98	97	96	96	95	95	94	94	93	93	13
14	102	101	100	99	99	98	97	96	96	95	95	94	94	14
15	103	102	102	101	100	99	98	98	97	96	96	95	95	15
16	105	104	103	102	102	101	100	99	98	98	97	96	96	16
17	106	105	105	104	103	102	101	101	100	99	98	98	97	17
18	108	107	106	105	105	104	103	102	101	101	100	99	98	18
19	109	108	107	107	106	105	104	104	103	102	101	100	100	19
20	111	110	109	108	107	107	106	105	104	104	103	102	101	20
21	112	111	110	110	109	108	107	106	106	105	104	103	102	21
22	114	113	112	111	110	109	109	108	107	106	105	105	104	22
23	115	114	113	113	112	111	110	109	108	108	107	106	105	23
24	117	116	115	114	113	112	112	111	110	109	108	107	107	24
25	119	118	117	116	115	114	113	112	112	111	110	109	108	25
26	120	119	119	118	117	116	115	114	113	112	111	111	110	26
27	122	121	120	119	119	118	117	116	115	114	113	112	111	27
28	123	123	122	121	120	119	119	118	117	116	115	114	113	28
29	125	124	124	123	122	121	120	120	119	118	117	116	115	29
30	128	127	126	124	124	123	122	122	121	120	119	118	117	30
31		130	129	127	126	125	124	123	123	122	121	120	119	31
32					129	128	127	126	125	124	123	122	122	32
33								129	128	127	126	125	124	33
34											130	129	127	34
35														35
36														36
37														37
38														38
39														39
40	Award 131 for all scores in this area													40
	6:1	6:2	6:3	6:4	6:5	6:6	6:7	6:8	6:9	6:10	6:11	7:0	7:1	

Raw score	\multicolumn{13}{c	}{Age in years and completed months}	Raw score
	7:2	7:3	7:4	7:5	7:6	7:7	7:8	7:9	7:10	7:11	8:0	8:1	8:2	
1	\multicolumn{13}{c	}{Award 69 for all scores in this area}	1
2														2
3														3
4	71	70	70											4
5	73	73	72	72	71	71	70	70						5
6	76	75	75	74	73	73	72	72	71	70	70			6
7	80	79	78	77	76	75	74	74	73	72	72	71	71	7
8	83	82	81	80	79	78	77	76	75	74	74	73	72	8
9	85	85	83	82	81	80	79	78	77	76	75	75	74	9
10	87	86	86	85	84	83	82	81	80	79	78	77	76	10
11	89	88	87	86	86	85	84	83	82	81	80	79	78	11
12	90	90	89	88	87	87	86	85	84	83	82	81	80	12
13	92	91	90	90	89	88	87	87	86	85	85	83	82	13
14	93	93	92	91	90	90	89	88	87	87	86	85	85	14
15	94	94	93	92	92	91	90	90	89	88	87	87	86	15
16	95	95	94	94	93	92	92	91	90	90	89	88	87	16
17	96	96	95	95	94	93	93	92	92	91	90	90	89	17
18	97	97	96	96	95	94	94	93	93	92	92	91	90	18
19	99	98	97	97	96	95	95	94	94	93	93	92	91	19
20	100	100	99	98	97	97	96	95	95	94	94	93	93	20
21	102	101	100	99	98	98	97	96	96	95	95	94	94	21
22	103	102	101	101	100	99	98	98	97	96	96	95	95	22
23	105	104	103	102	101	101	100	99	98	97	97	96	96	23
24	106	105	104	104	103	102	101	101	100	99	98	97	97	24
25	107	107	106	105	104	104	103	102	101	100	100	99	98	25
26	109	108	107	107	106	105	104	104	103	102	101	100	100	26
27	111	110	109	108	107	107	106	105	104	104	103	102	101	27
28	112	112	111	110	109	108	107	107	106	105	104	104	103	28
29	114	113	113	112	111	110	109	108	108	107	106	105	105	29
30	116	115	115	114	113	112	111	110	109	109	108	107	106	30
31	119	118	117	116	115	114	113	112	112	111	110	109	108	31
32	121	120	119	118	117	117	116	115	114	113	112	111	110	32
33	123	122	122	121	120	119	118	117	117	116	115	114	113	33
34	126	125	124	123	123	122	121	120	119	119	118	117	116	34
35		130	128	127	126	125	124	123	122	122	121	120	119	35
36						130	129	128	127	125	124	124	123	36
37												130	129	37
38														38
39														39
40	\multicolumn{13}{c	}{Award 131 for all scores in this area}	40
	7:2	7:3	7:4	7:5	7:6	7:7	7:8	7:9	7:10	7:11	8:0	8:1	8:2	

GaPS 2 Spring: Age-standardised scores

Raw score	6:5	6:6	6:7	6:8	6:9	6:10	6:11	7:0	7:1	7:2	7:3	7:4	7:5	7:6	7:7	Raw score
1	Award 69 for all scores in this area															1
2																2
3	70															3
4	74	73	72	71	71	70										4
5	77	76	76	75	74	73	72	71	71	70						5
6	80	79	78	77	76	76	75	74	73	72	71	71	70			6
7	82	81	80	79	79	78	77	76	76	75	74	73	72	71	71	7
8	83	83	82	81	81	80	79	78	77	77	76	75	74	73	73	8
9	85	84	84	83	82	82	81	80	79	78	78	77	76	75	75	9
10	87	86	85	85	84	83	82	82	81	80	79	79	78	77	76	10
11	88	87	87	86	85	85	84	83	82	82	81	80	79	79	78	11
12	90	89	88	87	86	86	85	84	84	83	82	82	81	80	79	12
13	91	90	90	89	88	87	86	86	85	84	83	83	82	81	81	13
14	93	92	91	90	89	88	87	87	86	85	85	84	83	83	82	14
15	94	93	92	92	91	90	89	88	87	87	86	85	84	84	83	15
16	95	94	93	93	92	91	90	90	89	88	87	86	86	85	84	16
17	96	95	95	94	93	93	92	91	90	89	88	87	87	86	85	17
18	98	97	96	95	94	94	93	92	91	91	90	89	88	87	86	18
19	99	98	97	96	95	95	94	93	93	92	91	90	89	88	87	19
20	100	100	99	98	97	96	95	94	94	93	92	91	91	90	89	20
21	102	101	100	99	98	97	96	95	95	94	93	93	92	91	90	21
22	103	102	101	101	100	99	98	97	96	95	94	94	93	92	92	22
23	104	104	103	102	101	100	99	98	97	96	95	95	94	93	93	23
24	106	105	104	103	102	101	101	100	99	98	97	96	95	94	94	24
25	108	107	106	105	104	103	102	101	100	99	98	97	96	96	95	25
26	109	108	107	106	105	104	103	103	102	101	100	99	98	97	96	26
27	110	109	109	108	107	106	105	104	103	102	101	101	100	99	98	27
28	113	111	110	109	109	108	107	106	105	104	103	102	101	100	100	28
29	114	113	112	111	110	109	108	108	107	105	105	104	103	102	101	29
30	116	115	114	113	112	111	110	109	108	108	106	105	105	104	103	30
31	118	117	116	115	114	113	112	111	110	109	108	108	107	106	105	31
32	120	120	119	118	116	115	115	114	113	112	110	109	109	108	107	32
33	122	122	121	120	119	118	117	116	115	114	113	112	111	110	109	33
34	124	124	123	122	121	121	120	119	118	117	116	115	114	113	112	34
35	129	127	126	124	124	123	122	122	121	120	119	118	117	116	115	35
36				130	129	127	126	124	124	123	122	122	121	120	119	36
37									130	129	127	125	124	124	123	37
38																38
39																39
40	Award 131 for all scores in this area															40
	6:5	6:6	6:7	6:8	6:9	6:10	6:11	7:0	7:1	7:2	7:3	7:4	7:5	7:6	7:7	

Raw score	Age in years and completed months												Raw score
	7:8	7:9	7:10	7:11	8:0	8:1	8:2	8:3	8:4	8:5	8:6	8:7	
1	Award 69 for all scores in this area												1
2													2
3													3
4													4
5													5
6													6
7	70												7
8	72	71	70										8
9	74	73	72	71	70	70							9
10	76	75	74	73	72	71	71	70					10
11	77	76	76	75	74	73	72	71	71	70			11
12	78	78	77	76	75	75	74	73	72	71	70	70	12
13	80	79	78	77	77	76	75	74	74	73	72	71	13
14	81	80	80	79	78	77	77	76	75	74	73	72	14
15	82	82	81	80	79	79	78	77	76	76	75	74	15
16	83	83	82	81	81	80	79	78	78	77	76	75	16
17	85	84	83	82	82	81	80	79	79	78	77	76	17
18	86	85	84	84	83	82	81	81	80	79	78	78	18
19	87	86	85	85	84	83	83	82	81	80	80	79	19
20	88	87	86	86	85	84	84	83	82	81	81	80	20
21	89	88	87	87	86	85	85	84	83	83	82	81	21
22	91	90	89	88	87	86	86	85	84	84	83	82	22
23	92	91	90	89	88	87	87	86	85	85	84	83	23
24	93	92	92	91	90	89	88	87	87	86	85	84	24
25	94	93	93	92	91	90	90	89	88	87	86	86	25
26	95	95	94	93	93	92	91	90	89	88	87	87	26
27	97	96	95	94	94	93	92	92	91	90	89	88	27
28	99	98	97	96	95	94	94	93	92	91	91	90	28
29	100	99	98	97	96	96	95	94	93	93	92	91	29
30	102	101	100	99	98	97	96	96	95	94	93	93	30
31	104	103	102	101	100	99	98	97	96	96	95	94	31
32	106	105	104	103	102	101	101	100	99	98	97	96	32
33	108	107	106	105	104	104	103	102	101	100	99	98	33
34	111	110	109	108	107	106	105	104	103	103	102	101	34
35	114	113	112	111	110	109	108	107	106	105	104	104	35
36	118	117	116	115	114	113	112	111	110	109	108	107	36
37	122	121	121	120	119	118	117	115	115	114	113	112	37
38	130	128	126	125	124	123	123	122	121	120	119	118	38
39												130	39
40	Award 131 for all scores in this area												40
	7:8	7:9	7:10	7:11	8:0	8:1	8:2	8:3	8:4	8:5	8:6	8:7	

GaPS 2 Spring: Age-standardised scores

GaPS 2 Summer: Age-standardised scores

Raw score	6:7	6:8	6:9	6:10	6:11	7:0	7:1	7:2	7:3	7:4	7:5	7:6	7:7	7:8	Raw score
1					Award 69 for all scores in this area										1
2															2
3															3
4	71	71	70	70											4
5	75	74	73	73	72	71	71	70							5
6	77	76	76	75	75	74	73	73	72	71	71	70			6
7	78	78	77	77	76	76	76	75	74	74	73	72	72	71	7
8	80	79	79	78	78	77	77	76	76	76	75	74	74	73	8
9	81	81	80	80	79	79	78	78	77	77	76	76	76	75	9
10	82	82	81	81	81	80	79	79	78	78	78	77	77	76	10
11	83	83	82	82	81	81	81	80	80	79	79	78	78	77	11
12	84	84	83	83	82	82	82	81	81	80	80	79	79	78	12
13	85	84	84	84	83	83	82	82	82	81	81	80	80	79	13
14	86	86	85	85	84	84	83	83	82	82	82	81	81	81	14
15	87	87	86	86	85	85	84	84	83	83	83	82	82	81	15
16	88	88	87	87	86	86	85	85	84	84	83	83	83	82	16
17	90	89	88	88	87	87	86	86	85	85	84	84	83	83	17
18	91	90	90	89	88	88	87	86	86	85	85	84	84	84	18
19	91	91	90	90	90	89	88	88	87	86	86	85	85	84	19
20	92	92	91	91	90	90	89	89	88	87	87	86	86	85	20
21	94	93	92	92	91	91	90	90	89	89	88	87	87	86	21
22	95	94	93	93	92	92	91	91	90	90	89	89	88	87	22
23	97	96	95	94	93	92	92	92	91	91	90	90	89	89	23
24	98	97	97	96	95	94	93	92	92	91	91	91	90	90	24
25	99	98	98	97	97	96	95	94	93	92	92	91	91	91	25
26	101	100	99	98	98	97	97	96	95	94	93	92	92	92	26
27	102	101	101	100	99	98	98	97	97	96	95	94	93	93	27
28	103	103	102	101	101	100	99	98	98	97	97	96	95	94	28
29	105	104	104	103	102	101	101	100	99	98	98	97	97	96	29
30	107	106	105	104	104	103	102	102	101	101	100	99	98	98	30
31	109	108	107	106	105	105	104	104	103	102	101	101	100	99	31
32	110	110	109	108	108	107	106	105	105	104	103	103	102	101	32
33	114	113	112	110	110	109	108	108	107	106	105	105	104	103	33
34	116	115	114	114	113	113	111	110	109	109	108	107	106	106	34
35	119	118	117	116	116	115	114	114	113	112	111	110	109	109	35
36	122	121	121	120	119	119	118	117	116	115	115	114	114	113	36
37	125	124	124	123	123	122	122	121	121	120	119	118	118	117	37
38					130	129	128	127	125	124	124	124	123	122	38
39															39
40					Award 131 for all scores in this area										40
	6:7	6:8	6:9	6:10	6:11	7:0	7:1	7:2	7:3	7:4	7:5	7:6	7:7	7:8	

Age in years and completed months

Raw score	7:9	7:10	7:11	8:0	8:1	8:2	8:3	8:4	8:5	8:6	8:7	8:8	8:9	8:10	Raw score
1					Award 69 for all scores in this area										1
2															2
3															3
4															4
5															5
6															6
7	70	70													7
8	72	72	71	70	70										8
9	74	74	73	72	72	71	70	70							9
10	76	75	75	74	73	73	72	71	71	70					10
11	77	76	76	76	75	74	74	73	72	72	71	70	70		11
12	78	77	77	77	76	76	75	75	74	73	72	72	71	70	12
13	79	79	78	78	77	77	76	76	75	75	74	73	73	72	13
14	80	80	79	79	78	78	77	77	76	76	75	75	74	73	14
15	81	81	80	80	79	79	78	78	77	77	76	76	75	75	15
16	82	81	81	81	80	80	79	79	78	78	77	77	76	76	16
17	83	82	82	81	81	81	80	80	79	79	78	78	77	77	17
18	83	83	82	82	82	81	81	80	80	80	79	79	78	78	18
19	84	84	83	83	82	82	82	81	81	80	80	79	79	79	19
20	85	84	84	84	83	83	82	82	82	81	81	80	80	79	20
21	86	85	85	84	84	84	83	83	82	82	82	81	81	80	21
22	87	86	86	85	85	84	84	84	83	83	82	82	82	81	22
23	88	87	87	86	86	85	85	84	84	83	83	83	82	82	23
24	89	89	88	87	87	86	86	85	85	84	84	83	83	83	24
25	90	90	89	89	88	87	87	86	86	85	85	84	84	83	25
26	91	91	90	90	89	89	88	87	87	86	86	85	85	84	26
27	92	92	91	91	90	90	89	89	88	87	87	86	86	85	27
28	94	93	92	92	91	91	90	90	89	89	88	87	87	86	28
29	96	95	94	93	92	92	91	91	91	90	90	89	88	88	29
30	97	97	96	95	94	93	92	92	92	91	91	90	90	89	30
31	99	98	97	97	96	96	95	94	93	92	92	91	91	91	31
32	101	100	99	98	98	97	97	96	96	95	94	93	92	92	32
33	103	102	101	101	100	99	98	98	97	97	96	96	95	94	33
34	105	104	104	103	102	102	101	100	100	99	98	98	97	97	34
35	108	107	106	106	105	104	104	103	102	102	101	100	100	99	35
36	112	111	110	109	109	108	107	106	105	105	104	104	103	102	36
37	116	115	115	114	114	113	112	110	110	109	109	108	107	106	37
38	122	121	121	120	119	119	118	117	116	115	115	114	114	113	38
39				130	129	128	127	126	125	124	124	123	123	122	39
40					Award 131 for all scores in this area										40
	7:9	7:10	7:11	8:0	8:1	8:2	8:3	8:4	8:5	8:6	8:7	8:8	8:9	8:10	

GaPS 2 Summer: Age-standardised scores